HOOKED

HKED

HOW LEADERS CONNECT, ENGAGE and INSPIRE with STORYTELLING

GABRIELLE DOLAN • YAMINI NAIDU

WILEY

First published in 2013 by John Wiley & Sons Australia, Ltd
42 McDougall St, Milton Qld 4064

Office also in Melbourne

Typeset in 11/13.5 pt ITC Giovanni Std Book

© One Thousand & One Pty Ltd

The moral rights of the authors have been asserted

National Library of Australia Cataloguing-in-Publication data:

Author:	Dolan, Gabrielle, author.
Title:	Hooked: how leaders connect, engage and inspire with storytelling/Gabrielle Dolan and Yamini Naidu.
ISBN:	9781118637623 (pbk.)
Notes:	Includes index.
Subjects:	Business communication.
	Business presentations.
	Oral interpretation.
	Storytelling.
	Success in business.
Other Authors/ Contributors:	Naidu, Yamini, author.
Dewey Number:	650.13

Cover design by Susan Olinsky

Author photo © Nathan Dyer

Social media icons © Orman Clark. www.premiumpixels.com

Printed in Singapore by C.O.S. Printers Pte Ltd

10 9 8 7 6 5 4 3 2

Disclaimer

CONTENTS

ABOUT THE AUTHORS

Gabrielle Dolan and Yamini Naidu are global thought leaders in storytelling and business communication.

Gabrielle has worked as an independent business management consultant and has held various senior leadership roles in change management, learning and development and project management. Her hands-on experience of the challenges leaders face in communicating effectively has led her to the power of storytelling. She is a sought-after keynote speaker and contributes articles on a regular basis to a variety of publications. Gabrielle holds a Master's degree in Management and Leadership from Swinburne University and an Associate Diploma in Education and Training from the University of Melbourne. Her current passion is in establishing her vegetable garden on her rural holiday property on the southern NSW coast where she goes often to stop and smell the roses ... well, the basil.

Yamini is an economist by training and a post graduate from the London School of Economics (LSE) and an LSE Scholarship winner. She grew up in Mumbai (Bombay), India, currently lives in Melbourne, Australia and has lived and worked in various parts of the world including Europe, Asia and America. She is an inspirational and highly sought-after keynote speaker and a prolific writer combining authenticity and humour with rich insights. She has held senior leadership roles and has extensive corporate experience working in a range of industry sectors with senior industry leaders, key stakeholders and company boards. Yamini is passionate about storytelling and through her work she inspires business leaders to experience business results using the power of storytelling. Outside work she is a serial yoga class attendee and a guide at the National Gallery of Victoria.

ACKNOWLEDGEMENTS

What gets us out of bed every morning, besides the alarm clock and our families, is the opportunity for us to do work we love, with people we like. Our clients allow us this luxury every day and they have been the inspiration for this book. We thank them for their support. It means the world to us.

Gabrielle says: I would specifically like to thank my husband Steve for your unwavering and continued support; and my gorgeous daughters, Alex and Jess, for keeping Mum grounded. I would also like to thank my parents, Margaret and Haydn, and my parents-in-law, Bill and Jan, as well as my wider family. I can always count on you for unconditional love and support and I hope I have made you proud. I am indebted to my very close friends, who have provided ongoing encouragement, inspiration and a lot of laughs along the way. Some of you have been on this journey with me literally every step of the way... you know who you are. Finally, I would like to thank my co-author and business partner, Yamini. I could not have done any of this without you and we have way too much fun together for this to be ever considered 'work'.

Yamini says: I would like to thank my wonderful husband Vishnu for your 100 per cent support, belief and pride in my work, and my beautiful daughter Tara for having humour, insight and compassion far beyond your years. You both light up my life. This book would not have been possible or worthwhile without your love and support. I am very grateful to all the wonderful people in my life: my parents Sundar and Rajalaxmi and my parents-in-law Jay and Kokila for their support, my brother Prathap, my sister Girija and my niece Poornima, who all 'get me', and still love me! I would not be the person I am without their influence in my life. A big thank you to my extended family and friends spread across the globe, particularly my besties, the 'gang of four', who have always provided me with endless love, encouragement, humour and inspiration. To Gabrielle, my business partner, thank you for your passion and commitment. It makes what we do amazing, exciting and fun.

Words cannot describe (but we are going to try anyway) the debt of gratitude we owe Peter Cook, our mentor, who introduced us to the concept of Thought Leadership. Peter, you constantly encourage us to push ourselves further, calmly ignoring our shouts of protest. You believed in us even before we did. Every coffee with you results in magic happening. It was over one of these coffees sprinkled with magic dust that we were introduced to Lucy Raymond from John Wiley & Sons.

We thank Lucy for not laughing outright at us when we met her for the very first time and modestly declared we had a bestseller on our hands, and for taking us on. Lucy and the whole team at Wiley, specifically Sandra Balonyi (editor extraordinaire), Keira de Hoog, Elizabeth Whiley, Katie Elliott and Gretta Blackwood, have all been a pleasure to work with. We soaked up their guidance and wisdom whenever we could.

We would like to thank Kelly Irwin, who showed tremendous fortitude by undertaking the initial editing process and did an amazing job in taking our concepts, ideas and random ramblings and putting them in a logical, cohesive sequence. She was the tough love we needed.

We would also like to thank our friends and colleagues at HubMelbourne, who energise us and support us every time we enter this amazing co-working space, particularly Ehon Chan and Jan Stewart, who make the Hub and the world a better place.

We would especially like to thank Robert Davis, who suggested the title *Hooked*. It was like having the dark clouds lift and a beam of sunlight hit us in the heart. We loved it instantly. Deepest thanks to Matt Church for imparting the wisdom of doing work we love with people we like and Michael Henderson who so generously gave of his expertise at very short notice to help us nail our back cover blurb.

We would also like to thank our first business coach, who has now become a life-long friend. Sandra Marks, we love the sanity check, wisdom and humour you bring into our lives.

Our gratitude to our fellow storytellers Steve Denning and Annette Simmons who paved the road for us and whose work inspires us.

We would also like to thank the thousands of leaders we have had the privilege and the pleasure to work with all over the world. It is through your enthusiasm to learn, your ability to challenge and your courage to try something new that we continue to enhance our knowledge and expertise in storytelling.

Just like you never forget your first love, you never forget your first client, so we would like to thank Kate Colley and Phil Davis for giving us our very first opportunity. We are both humbled and deeply grateful.

We would especially like to thank some very special clients who have been ongoing supporters and ambassadors for us. Sonia Aplin, Natalia Mina, Loredana Moretto, Jac Phillips and Jade Wisely, we have learned so much from you and it is a pleasure and an honour to work with you.

We would specifically like to thank all the leaders who agreed to have their stories shared in this book. Every leader we asked immediately agreed and your support and generosity deeply touched us. This book would not be the book it is without your stories.

Finally we would like to thank you, the reader, for picking up this book and daring to become the inspiring leader you can be.

To all of you we dedicate this book and acknowledge your role in making it happen.

Thank you,

Gabrielle and Yamini

INTRODUCTION

*Storytelling is the most powerful way to put
ideas into the world today.*

**Robert McKee, founder and
presenter of the Story Seminar**

Stories and storytelling can save you.

Stories can save you time and money by fast-tracking
trust — and sales — with your clients. Stories can save you
thousands of hours in team meetings that have no purpose
and little impact. Stories can help you nail that long-
awaited promotion and they can help you communicate
effectively, saving you your reputation and your company
millions of dollars.

Stories can save your relationships with long-standing
customers and they can add magic to potentially boring
presentations by making your PowerPoint slides meaningful
and purposeful.

When we first started out in our corporate careers, we were in
awe of leaders who possessed a natural ability to engage and
inspire us. When they presented, we sat up and listened. We
remembered what they said long after the event. When they
suggested a new path to go down, we followed. Why did we
have complete faith in their direction? What was their secret
sauce? And how could we get some too?

Flash forward to 2005, and there we were sitting on a park
bench one warm, sunny day in the heart of Melbourne's CBD

when it hit us: all inspiring leaders tell stories that break down emotional barriers and tap into what we think and feel. Their stories hook us in.

We began to imagine a world in which all business leaders didn't just use facts and numbers, but used facts, numbers and stories to connect, engage and inspire. This world is no longer a dream — it's a reality. In today's business world — in an age of information overload — it is no longer effective to 'just tell people the facts'. As a leader you must use emotion to be successful in business.

In his book *Business Stripped Bare*, Richard Branson explains why business and emotions go together. He writes: 'Engage your emotions at work. Your instincts and emotions are there to help you. They are there to make things easier'.

Back to 2005 ... We are still sitting on the bench having this 'aha' moment, which made us decide to leave the security, comfort and fortnightly salary of our respective employers and start a company that teaches, mentors and inspires CEOs, executives and leaders just like you to tell stories that get killer business results.

Since then we have worked with CEOs and senior leaders of large corporations, as well as small-business owners and entrepreneurs. We have run our workshops in organisations all over Australia and New Zealand, as well as New York, London and in the middle of a rice-paddy field in Indonesia (now *that* is a good story).

We are now ready to share our knowledge and experience — all that we have learned over this time. More importantly, we are ready to share what our clients have learned. In this book, you will find real-world, practical examples, actual stories leaders have shared, the successes they have had and their sheer determination to achieve. You will find all this and more — all designed to help you become a successful storyteller and leader in your field.

Whether you need to engage your employees to adopt your company's new strategy, become an inspiring presenter, attract new clients or win a lucrative contract, this book will show you how storytelling and stories can help you get there.

What we love most about business storytelling is how far and wide it can be applied. Storytelling can, and should, be used in presentations, sales pitches, team meetings and coaching sessions, as well as on your website, in emails and across all your social media platforms. After reading this book, you will no doubt find many more communication channels that you will want to apply storytelling to.

You will begin to notice how your day-to-day life experiences can become powerful business stories — from watching your children surf to trying to impress your partner's father. This is all rich material that you can use for your stories — and we will show you how.

The good news is that to human beings, storytelling comes naturally; it is something that we all already do. We have been sharing stories since the dawn of time — in cave paintings, around campfires, at bedtime and more. Importantly, we tend to remember stories.

Do you, for example, remember the age-old story, '1001 Arabian Nights'? We certainly do — it is the story that inspired our company's name.

The king in the story marries a new woman every day and has her killed the next day. The minister responsible for finding each new bride has a tough gig. If he does not find the king a wife, he himself will be killed. (And you thought you had tough deadlines!)

So the minister's brave daughter, Scheherazade, volunteers to be the king's next bride. On her wedding night, Scheherazade tells the king a long, wonderful story but stops right at the cliffhanger ending. The king is beside himself! He wants to know what happens next! Scheherazade tells him she is tired and she will continue the story the following night.

The next night comes and Scheherazade finishes that story and starts a new one. Again she stops right before the ending, telling the king she will finish it tomorrow.

This routine goes on for 1001 nights, by which time the king has not only let Scheherazade live, but also fallen deeply in love with her.

This story is quite possibly one of the first case studies that proves the power of storytelling. When mastered correctly, stories can change the way we think, feel and act.

This book will show you how to use powerful stories in a business context. It will help you to:

- build strong relationships with existing and potential clients, customers and employees
- communicate effectively with everyone around you
- influence and inspire others to take action
- engage Gen Y clients, customers and employees
- illustrate your points and sell your services, ideas or products
- keep ahead of your peers, colleagues and customers
- motivate and influence your team to new heights
- hook your audience in
- kill your competition.

At the end of most chapters we throw you an optional mission (we call these 'How hooked are you?'). They may involve thinking about your current practices or starting to craft your own stories. Of course, they are *your* missions and you can choose whether or not to accept them.

As old Hopi wisdom says, 'The one who tells the stories, rules the world'.

So are you ready to rule your world?

CHAPTER 1
What is business storytelling?

Storytelling can be used to persuade, motivate, and inspire in ways that cold facts, bullet points and directives can't.

Annette Simmons, author of *The Story Factor*

When we started our business in 2005, the term 'business storytelling', or 'organisational storytelling', was nowhere to be seen. It was not bandied about on business websites, on blogs or in the media. It wasn't even on Wikipedia. So we came up with our own definition:

Business storytelling is sharing a story about an experience, but linking it to a business message that will influence and inspire your audience into action.

Like traditional storytelling, business storytelling tells a story, but unlike traditional stories, business stories carry a message to connect, inspire and engage an audience.

In this chapter we will explore the difference between traditional storytelling and business storytelling. We will also look at how metaphors and analogies differ from stories.

A story about storytelling

The definition we gave earlier is one that we came up with and to demonstrate what we mean, we are going to tell you a story. After all, this wouldn't be a book on storytelling if we didn't! We will set up the context of the story before actually sharing the story.

The context

Michael Brandt was Regional Executive at National Australia Bank. Michael was responsible for 16 branches and in every team in every branch he had the same problem: his team members did not meet their weekly targets for sales leads to the sales department — known as quality sales leads.

He held countless meetings where he talked to his teams about this issue and tried to coach them on the importance of referring leads to the sales team. At every meeting, Michael's team members reiterated that they understood their targets and knew what had to be done. Yet most of them failed to meet their targets — even when they were linked to their annual performance bonus.

Michael was at the end of his tether. He had tried everything he could think of over a period of 12 months. His frustration was tangible, and you can imagine how frustrating it must have been for his team members. Michael constantly asked them why they weren't meeting their targets. Why were the majority unable to achieve their weekly sales-leads targets?

Then one day they said to him, 'It's the one thing we hate doing. Every Monday when we come in to work we think, "Oh no, not weekly sales-leads targets again"'.

Michael came to our workshop and said, 'I've tried everything for a year to help my team achieve their quality sales-leads targets and nothing has worked'.

So during one of our workshops, Michael constructed the following story.

The brussels sprouts story

When I was a kid, I hated brussels sprouts. Every time brussels sprouts were served at dinner, I always left them until last, hoping I would get away with not eating them. But, of course, my mother would never let me leave the table until I ate my brussels sprouts ... every last one.

One evening, when brussels sprouts were served yet again, I decided to eat my brussels sprouts first. Then I relaxed and enjoyed the rest of my meal.

Do you think we could treat our quality sales leads like brussels sprouts? None of us can leave the table unless we have eaten our brussels sprouts. Do you think we could eat them quickly and early in the week so that we can all relax and enjoy the rest of the week?

The results

A few weeks after our workshop, we saw Michael at a follow-up session. He told us that 11 of the 16 branches where he had visited and narrated his brussels sprouts story had achieved their sales-leads targets for two continuous weeks. It was the first time in a year that this had happened. And the only thing he had done differently was tell that story. He even told us that the term 'brussels sprouts' had become a shorthand motivator within the teams. Now his team members were asking each other, 'How many brussels sprouts have you eaten? I've already eaten three today and it's not even lunchtime!'

The story Michael used linked an everyday experience to a business message that achieved significant measurable results. That is the powerful impact business stories can have! The good news is that you already use storytelling. When you talk about the coffee you had yesterday, your last holiday or a recent meeting with a client, you are telling a story. People tell stories naturally, intuitively, organically because we are hardwired to do so. This means that we are hardwired to listen to stories too. This is great news for you as a leader because it means that your audience are ready and willing participants. People are eager to listen to — and love hearing — well-told, short, purposeful stories.

Stories are how we think. They are how we make meaning of life. Call them schemas, scripts, cognitive maps, mental models, metaphors or narratives. Stories are how we explain how things work, how we make decisions, how we justify our decisions, how we persuade others, how we understand our place in the world, create our identities, and define and teach social values.

Dr Pamela Rutledge, Director, Media Psychology Research Center

Even after his passing, Steve Jobs continues to inspire and engage us through his stories. We are hooked on Steve Jobs's stories: both the stories surrounding his life and the stories he shared with his listeners.

In Walter Isaacson's best-selling biography *Steve Jobs* there is a story that Jobs used to explain his own perfectionist streak.

> ### The Steve Jobs story
>
> As a young boy, Jobs had helped his father build a fence around their backyard, and he was told they had to use just as much care on the back of the fence as on the front.
>
> 'Nobody will ever know,' young Steve said. His father replied, 'But *you* will know. A true craftsman uses a good piece of wood even for the back of a cabinet against the wall,' his father explained, 'and they should do the same for the back of the fence'. It was the mark of an artist to have such a passion for perfection.
>
> Jobs inherited that passion. His engineers at Apple were expected to place the chips inside the motherboard of every computer in a perfectly straight line.
>
> 'Nobody is going to see the PC board,' one of them protested. Jobs reacted as his father had: 'I want it to be as beautiful as possible, even if it's inside the box. A great carpenter isn't going to use lousy wood for the back of a cabinet, even though nobody's going to see it'.

Storytelling in business is not only the stories you share as a leader — such as Michael's brussels sprouts story — but also the stories that are shared about you, such as the Steve Jobs story. As a leader you need to be aware that both exist and both are powerful.

The buzz on business storytelling

There is a very big difference between storytelling in business and the storytelling you use at home with your friends and family to explain what Aunt Cecilia did yesterday or what happened on your last big holiday overseas. So it is time for some tough love: the truth is that not everyone who tells stories can do it successfully in business. The trick is to master the difference between storytelling and storytelling in a business context.

If you think of storytelling across a spectrum, then business storytelling is at one end of the spectrum and traditional storytelling — the stuff you tell at home, in the pub or with family and friends — is at the other. Traditional storytelling is like life before Google; business storytelling is like life after Google. They really are very different!

There are three reasons why business storytelling is different from other forms of storytelling. Business stories:

- *have a purpose,* whether it is to sell your product or announce your company's new strategic direction
- *are supported by data*
- *are authentic* — true stories that relate back to your purpose.

Let's look at each of these in turn.

Purpose

A business story must have a purpose. What is the point of the story? What is the message you are trying to get across to your audience? In our personal life (traditional storytelling), we often tell stories that have no point except to get a laugh, share information or relay experiences. That's fine and appropriate in that context, but in business you have to emit a laser-beam-like focus on your purpose. We show you how to nail your purpose in chapter 4, but for now take a look at this example.

Matt Ritchie is the National Manager in Sales Strategy and Delivery at MLC Australia. Matt needed a story that would inspire his team to think differently about customer service. This is the story he shared.

Bruce Springsteen and customer service

I was recently reading a magazine that featured an interview with Bruce Springsteen. Bruce Springsteen has been a musician and performer for more than 20 years and has a tremendous reputation as a live act.

When he was asked how he remains motivated night after night to perform at his best, he replied that while every night is a 'Bruce Springsteen concert night' to him, the audience have most likely paid money to see a Bruce Springsteen concert for the first — and possibly only — time in their lives. He added that wanting to give them the best-ever Bruce Springsteen experience is what makes him enthusiastic night after night.

Reading that article reminded me of all of us at work every day. While we might take hundreds of calls from hundreds of customers every day, one of those calls will be from a customer who has never called us before and who may never call us again, depending on our response. It might be the only contact they ever have with MLC. It might be the only 'Bruce Springsteen concert' they ever go to. Imagine the difference we could make if each and every customer, each and every time they call, got the full 'Bruce Springsteen experience'.

Matt's purpose was to inspire his team to think about customer service in a different way. With this purpose in mind he shared a personal experience and linked it to a business message.

How did this story make you feel? It sure struck a chord with everyone in Matt's audience. After reading the story, do you understand how customer service is to be delivered in this organisation? Does it make you want to deliver it in the way Matt describes? Would you remember this story? Do you think you could and would retell it to others?

These are your aims when you are communicating a story to your employees, clients, potential clients and all of your stakeholders. As Dan and Chip Heath suggest in their best-selling book, *Made to Stick: Why Some Ideas Survive and Others Die*, ask yourself the following three questions about your audience:

- Do they understand what I have just said?
- Can they remember it?
- Can they retell it without losing its meaning?

We have seen client after client use purposeful storytelling to successfully address these three challenges.

Data

The second difference between storytelling at the water cooler and storytelling in the boardroom is that in the boardroom you have to take a hard-nosed business approach to storytelling. That means you can never present in a fairy outfit or start a story with 'Once upon a time' — not that there is anything wrong with that, if your audience is under five.

When you use stories to pitch for work or present as a keynote speaker at an event, you have to include the hard facts, data and figures, and support this data with stories.

When we present about our business, we use the employee engagement scores that we have lifted, case studies and other evaluation results that show how we have helped our clients succeed. We then bring this data alive using stories. The stories we tell make the intangible, tangible. They explain the data and information in a way that is memorable and engaging. Stories hook your audience to your data. Data alone is hard to understand, remember and retell (thus failing to address the three challenges that Dan and Chip Heath pose).

Storytelling is a crucial tool for management and leadership, because often, nothing else works. Charts leave listeners bemused. Prose remains unread. Dialogue is just too laborious and slow. Time after time, when faced with the task of persuading a group of managers or front-line staff in a large organisation to get enthusiastic about a major change, storytelling is the only thing that works.

Steve Denning, organisational storyteller and author

We are here to set you up for success and we would never suggest that all you need is stories. You will never hear us say fluffy things such as 'Just find the narrative' or 'Just tell your brand story or leadership story'. Instead, repeat after us: 'In business storytelling, your stories support your data'. But most leaders just stop with data, and this limits, or even hinders, their success. Why? Because just sticking with the facts is doing things the old way and will bore your audience into a coma. The important thing you need to do as a leader is to bring the facts to life using stories. Stories help you connect, engage and inspire your audience, which data simply cannot do.

Maybe stories are just data with a soul.

Brené Brown, *The Power of Vulnerability* (TED Talks video)

Of course, your data will vary depending on what you do and the industry in which you do it. Data may be a report, a business case, a cost–benefit analysis, research, statistics, an implementation plan or a Gantt chart. You may find your data exciting, but rest assured most of your audience will not. So just providing this information is not enough to get people hooked on what you are saying.

In the past, leaders presented only the facts, figures and data. But this is often difficult for an audience to understand, remember and retell—which is your aim. And there's a flipside to the coin too: stories without data are all sizzle and no steak. Have a look at figure 1.1 for a diagrammatic representation of how the combination of data and stories will get your audience hooked.

Figure 1.1: data + story model

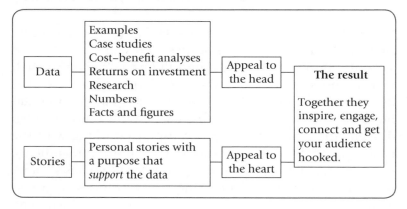

Very few leaders use both data and stories and even fewer do it in an inspiring way. So the minute you can do both, you will enjoy far greater success. In sales, you will move straight out in front of your competitors and in leadership you will have a positive impact on your employees and your personal leadership brand.

Authenticity

The third difference between a business story and a traditional story is that in business all the stories you tell must be true.

Do you remember the controversy over the book *A Million Little Pieces* by James Frey? It was promoted by Oprah Winfrey's book club and became an instant hit. James Frey presented his book as a non-fiction memoir of his years as a drug addict, alcoholic and criminal. Later it was revealed that the author had wildly embellished and fabricated parts of the book. The book was then mocked as 'A Million Little Lies'.

Frey appeared again on Oprah Winfrey's show and admitted he had not been truthful in the book. Winfrey said, 'I feel duped. But more importantly, I feel that you betrayed millions of readers'.

We cannot stress enough how important it is for you in business to ensure all the stories you tell are authentic. If you do not and people find out the truth, it will have a negative backlash on your reputation.

If you are still not convinced of this, think about these two words: 'Lance' and 'Armstrong'. After being stripped of his seven Tour de France titles Armstrong continued to plead his innocence. In January 2013, Armstrong finally admitted to using drugs throughout his professional cycling career. This came after years of denying allegations and telling stories that were simply not true. By his own admission he will now spend the rest of his life trying to recover his credibility.

If you were an Armstrong fan, do you remember how you felt when he admitted this? Or can you think of another time you were told a story that you later found out was not true? Did you feel duped, or betrayed, or angry... or all three? For your business storytelling to be successful, everything about it has to be authentic. You absolutely do not want a James Frey or a Lance Armstrong moment in your professional life.

Metaphors and analogies

It is worth spending just a bit of time on metaphors and analogies as we are often asked, 'Are they the same as stories?' The answer is, 'No, they are not!'

(continued)

Metaphors and analogies (cont'd)

A story has a beginning, a middle and an ending. It is about a specific event and it has emotion (makes your audience feel something) and sensory data (paints a picture for your audience). A metaphor or analogy usually just paints a picture or gives your audience an easy way of understanding something.

Technically there is a difference between metaphors and analogies but for simplicity we will treat them as the same. They both provide your audience with an easy way of comparing something. For example, Shakespeare famously said, 'All the world's a stage' and Forrest Gump equally profoundly said, 'My momma always said, "Life was like a box of chocolates. You never know what you're gonna get"'.

Metaphors and analogies work when you are trying to get people to grasp a difficult concept. They work particularly well when you are trying to educate people. Quite often trainers and teachers will use a lot of metaphors and analogies.

For example, a metaphor is useful for explaining the difference between a bull and a bear market: think of a bear market as a bear clawing prices down with its claws and think of a bull market as a bull tossing prices up with its horns. Simple and easy to remember!

A word of caution: metaphors and analogies do not necessarily inspire and engage your audience. A mistake people can make with analogies is to use an analogy that in itself needs explaining. Remember that the reason for using an analogy is to help people better understand something. So if your analogy poses more questions than answers, don't use it.

Take, for example, the rather useless analogy made by an industry expert in 2008 when BHP was bidding to take over Rio Tinto. The expert described the situation as two giants fighting in a jungle, adding that it would be best to sit back and watch as no-one knows what may fall off the back of a truck.

This analogy was ridiculed in national newspapers as it did nothing to help people understand what this expert was trying to say. It only posed more questions, such as what the giants were doing in the jungle, who was driving the truck and what exactly was on the truck that could fall off! It was an analogy that did not help clarify the message.

So metaphors and analogies have a purpose, but they are not stories. We suggest using a combination: a metaphor or an analogy where appropriate (when you want to give your audience a quick way of understanding something) and stories to connect, engage and inspire.

We hope you are now excited by the possibilities of what storytelling can do for you when it is purposeful, authentic and supported by data and that you realise that people who use only analogies and metaphors are paddling a canoe up a creek without an oar.

In a nutshell

Did you get hooked?

→ Business storytelling is different from traditional storytelling because in business your stories have a purpose; are supported by data; and are authentic, true stories that relate back to your purpose.

→ Stories help you meet the three vital challenges of communicating as a leader:

  – Can people understand what you are saying?

  – Can they remember the story?

  – Can they retell it?

  Data alone cannot do this.

→ A story is not the same as a metaphor or an analogy. Metaphors and analogies provide your audience with an easy way to compare something but do not necessarily engage or inspire.

→ Beware the metaphor or analogy that itself needs further explanation.

→ In a business context you need to use a combination of metaphors, analogies and stories, as appropriate: metaphors and analogies when you want to give your audience a quick way of understanding something, and stories to connect, engage and inspire.

How hooked are you?

As a leader, what do you think are some points from this chapter that you could use the next time you are in front of an audience? What about other leaders you admire: are they using any of the ideas in this chapter?

Now that you understand the concept of business storytelling, read the next chapter to discover the importance of storytelling in a business context.

CHAPTER 2
The importance of business storytelling

Stories are the single most powerful weapon in a leader's arsenal.

Howard Gardner, Harvard University

In this chapter we explore how business storytelling can help you with the challenges of being a leader in the 21st century.

We also look at the importance of emotion in leadership and how you can make emotion work for you; the importance of personal credibility; and we will introduce you to the concept of 'the curse of knowledge'. (Don't panic! We will explain what this is shortly.)

Face the facts: times have changed

When we speak to leaders about using storytelling in business, they often say, 'I knew it — I knew there was something I was missing!' In leadership, that good-old, military-style command and control where you just tell people what to do and give them the facts — and whatever you ask for is simply done — doesn't work anymore, no matter how much we wish it would!

Too often, leaders fall into the trap of thinking people will automatically listen to them and take appropriate, effective action in response to what they expect just because of their authoritative position. They soon learn that leading others is much more complicated than that. People are much more complicated than that. Even in the military, communication and leadership are the two biggest challenges leaders face every day.

Leadership has moved from 'command and control' to what organisational storyteller and author Steve Denning describes as 'engage and enrol'.

In today's age of information overload and with information being at everyone's fingertips, you as a leader can no longer provide only information. Instead, you must learn how to engage and enrol everyone around you in the information.

Given the unfathomable sea of information afforded us through the internet, storytelling is an invaluable resource as it provides the means for delivering substance and meaning in a form that can be readily grasped by the masses.

Jon Hansen, Harvard University

Whether it is to create buy-in for your company's new strategy, new corporate principles, an upcoming business change or a new product, the simplest and most powerful way to win over your audience is by telling an authentic story that creates meaning and connection. We have witnessed this over and over again with clients in a variety of industries within a variety of sectors all over the world. We know that storytelling works.

Of course, for storytelling to be effective it has to be executed correctly. That is possibly one of the reasons why you picked up this book and we will show you how to do this throughout the book.

Only dinosaurs stick with facts

To succeed as a leader today, you must add storytelling to your repertoire and skill set. It is an essential business skill.

If you think that as a leader your job is limited to passing on information, then you are competing with Google and — guess what? — you will never win that competition! The role of the leader as purely an information provider will soon be extinct (if it isn't already). The new role of leaders is to make information relevant, meaningful and engaging, and what better way to do that than through storytelling?

Throughout your business career, you have probably been told many times, 'Just stick to the facts'. It's what we were taught to do and expected to do. There is little wonder then that the vast majority of businesspeople rely heavily on just the facts when they communicate. You have probably worked to that same mentality yourself. We know we have certainly been guilty of this.

The other downside of using just the facts is that facts and data are hard to remember because they lack emotion. It is very hard to get people hooked on just the facts. Now please don't get us wrong: we are *not* saying 'dump the facts'. What we are saying is that you cannot influence, persuade, connect and inspire with just the facts.

Logic makes people think, but it is emotion that makes people act.

Zig Ziglar, author and motivational speaker

So, what do you need in addition to the facts?

Besides the facts — and logic — as a leader you have to create an emotional connection to yourself and your message. You have to tap into emotions. Harvard Business School professor and award-winning author John Kotter presents us with a valuable insight: 'Behaviour change happens mostly by speaking to people's feelings'.

Show me the love

By now, you are probably scared. If you've been taught to just tell the facts, you could be running for the hills. For decades, leaders have shied away from using emotion in business. We were ignorant about the power of emotion in business for a whole lot of reasons — for example, beliefs such as 'It's business; don't make it personal'.

We would like to tell you about a leader who overcame these barriers and tapped into emotion using storytelling. Let us introduce you to Darren Whitelaw — Director of Corporate Communications at Department of Planning and Community Development in Victoria, Australia — who wanted all his leaders to have more face-to-face conversations with their teams instead of always sending out emails. Makes sense, right? This is the story he told.

Only the real thing will do

Last month, I had the opportunity to travel overseas and was looking forward to it as it would be a break from my usual routine. When I was overseas, my wife set up our laptop on my daughter's breakfast table and I talked to my daughter daily via webcam. My wife told me that once, when the laptop was lying shut on the sofa, my daughter picked it up, hugged it and said, 'Daddy'. That moved me in such a way that I realised sometimes in life you can substitute the real thing, but sometimes only the real thing will do.

I am sharing this with you as it reminds us that every day we have that same choice as leaders and communicators. We can send out emails or we can go out and talk to our people face to face — because sometimes only the real thing will do.

How did this story make you feel? Are you getting on the phone to make time for face-to-face meetings yet?

People buy on emotion and justify on logic. If you work in sales, you may already be aware of this concept. As a leader, this is important to understand and embrace, as every leader is the biggest salesperson any company has. In your role as a leader you need to rally up the workforce, your customers and your clients and get them to buy into a new strategic direction, a new way of working or a new way of thinking. Emotion persuades others to make decisions. To buy or not to buy? That is the question — whether that's to buy your product or to buy into your idea or new strategy.

Tapping into emotions does not mean you have to make your team weep into buckets as they implement the next service-level agreement. What we're talking about is a healthy range of emotions that are appropriate in a work context, such as the feeling of pride in a job well done or the feeling that something is not fair. We will show you in chapter 5 what level of emotion is appropriate in storytelling and how to include this safely when you are storytelling so that it works for you and your audience. For now, suffice to say that emotions are important in business, and storytelling is one of the ways you can make emotions work for you.

When dealing with people, remember you are not dealing with creatures of logic, but creatures of emotion.

Dale Carnegie, *How to Win Friends and Influence People*

No matter how much we would like to believe we are rational creatures who occasionally act emotionally, the truth is we are actually emotional beings who occasionally act rationally. We know that sounds scary, but you just have to look at the stockmarkets, the consumer confidence index and people's behaviour in general to know this is true.

Emotions are essential in leadership and in business because they do two powerful things for you: they help you remember and they help you take action.

Can you remember where you were and what you were doing when you heard the news that Princess Diana had died? What about when 9/11 happened? We remember these stories because we had such a strong emotional reaction to what we were experiencing.

Emotion helps people remember and emotion is the catalyst for action — that's why, as a leader, you have to tap into emotion. One of the simple, yet powerful, ways of doing this is through a story because at the core of every story is emotion.

One leader we worked with was faced with the challenge of convincing her business unit that continually striving to attract and retain good employees was becoming ever more important. (Consultancy company McKinsey & Co termed this 'the war for talent'.) This is an adaptation of the story she told. She taps into emotion to help her audience remember and take action.

The milk crates

When I was about 14 my dad took me to the football every week. We would stand in the outer and, being smaller than everyone else, I often missed out on seeing the action. One week we decided to bring along an old milk crate we had lying around to stand on. It was great — I was finally ahead of everyone else and could watch the whole game. The next week we brought along the milk crate again, but this time we noticed that a few other people had also brought their milk crates. We were actually a bit impressed that we had started a trend. Unfortunately, within a few months nearly everyone had a milk crate and I was literally back to square one, back with the rest of the pack.

My experience at those matches reminds me of what we are trying to achieve with the war for talent. We can't be happy with starting a trend and taking an early lead; we need to constantly be on the lookout for our next milk crate.

To connect, engage and inspire as a leader you have to learn how to make emotion work for you — not against you — and how to use storytelling as a tool to do that.

Credibility is critical

Along with facts, logic and emotion you also need to have credibility. As a leader, you need to have a certain amount of credibility before your audience will believe you. They have to trust you before they can trust your message.

Research titled 'Building Trust in Business 2012' indicates that trust is not only nice to have, it is a commercial imperative. This research, conducted on trust and leadership, surveyed

440 leaders at more than 300 companies globally. The results show a clear, explicit connection between companies that achieve strong business results and high ratings in trust, leadership and collaboration.

While trust and credibility are usually built up over time, there are times when, as a leader, you have to fast-track these. This applies every time you lead a new team or new team members join your team. It also applies every time you walk into a job interview and every time you are in front of people giving a presentation or sales pitch.

We are not suggesting that you are not trustworthy, nor that you don't have credibility, but just as you have to continually work on personal fitness, you have to continually work on keeping the credibility you have earned. This is crucial in business and essential in times of change and uncertainty. Without doubt the best way to do this is through your actions and decisions. Your actions will always speak louder than words. The second-best way is through the appropriate use of stories.

To be persuasive, we must be believable; to be believable, we must be credible; to be credible, we must be truthful.

Edward R. Murrow, American broadcast journalist

One of our clients, Rob Jager, was Shell New Zealand's Country Chair. Rob was new to the role and he told us that one of the key messages he wanted to get across was, 'Spend Shell money as if it is your own'. But he was new to the job. Why should his people trust him and his message? It could be that he was just pushing another company line. We asked him why this message was important to him and he shared this story.

> ### Spending money wisely
>
> When I was a kid, we weren't rich and we certainly weren't poor, but my parents worked full time and they would always say to me and my two brothers, 'You work hard for your money, but you only get to spend it once, so spend it wisely'. That has always stayed with me and it is something I value.

We then asked Rob if he had ever shared that story with any of his employees and — guess what? — he hadn't. So Rob started sharing the story as part of his 'Spend Shell money as if it is your own' message and he started to experience a far better response.

Rob was attempting to influence purely through logic. 'Spend Shell money as if it was your own' was just a bland statement. Through the story of his childhood he earned credibility that the message actually did mean something to him and that it wasn't just another cost-cutting drive. The personal story also created an emotional connection to the message. On hearing that story you may have thought about your parents giving you similar advice.

The winning trifecta

So far we have explored how you need logic, how you need to create an emotional connection and how you need credibility as a leader in business. And you do need all three.

Aristotle's model of influence

The Greek philosopher Aristotle first put the three main forms of influence — logos (logic), ethos (personal credibility or character) and pathos (emotional connection) — together in a model. The model is approximately 2500 years old, but it has stood the test of time. If it had been a matrix, Aristotle could have laid claim to being the first ever consultant.

Logic

Logic — or logos — is the data, the facts and the figures as well as the business reasons your audience need to see and hear.

Personal credibility

Personal credibility — or ethos — is the degree of trust-worthiness and credibility you have in your audience's eyes regarding the messages you are delivering. Please note that this is not about positional credibility (credibility that comes from holding a position in an organisation). This is about personal credibility — you the person and how credible you are in the eyes of your audience.

The CEO of a company has positional credibility, but they may not have personal credibility. For example, when John Fletcher was appointed CEO of Coles Myer — one of Australia's biggest retailers — he admitted that he 'hadn't set foot in a supermarket for 25 years', destroying any personal credibility in the eyes of his employees and stakeholders.

Emotional connection

Emotional connection — or pathos — is the extent to which your audience connects to you and your message. When you're trying to inspire an employee to embrace a new idea, or a client to buy your products or services, you have to create an emotional connection.

Using the model to influence

What does this model mean for you in business? If you look at the ways people tend to communicate in business, about

90 per cent of the time we operate in the 'logic' space. We use facts, figures, measures, return on investment, reasons why we need to change and benefits — and we pull all of this data together in a spreadsheet, pie chart or PowerPoint presentation. We are not saying that facts are not important. They absolutely are. What we are saying (and this is a moot point) is that facts inform — they don't influence.

If logic alone were enough, no-one would smoke cigarettes or speed while driving. We would all exercise and eat right every day, our customers would buy our products over those of our competitors, our staff would embrace every change we make and our kids would do everything we say. Yeah, right!

To influence successfully as a leader you need to also look at the other two elements in Aristotle's model. As a 21st century leader you first need to use ethos to get your audience to trust you. You then have to find the right emotion (pathos) to tap into so your audience gets your message. As a leader you need ethos and pathos to sell yourself and your messages. Remember that when we talk about selling we are not just talking about selling in the traditional sense of products and services to customers. We are also talking about how, as a leader, you sell yourself, your leadership, your strategy, your vision or your great idea to your employees and other stakeholders.

Today, people need to feel they can trust their leaders. They want to build a connection with you. We are not suggesting you should throw logic out the window. We are saying that you need to integrate all three of the main forms of influence: personal credibility, emotional connection and sound logic.

As a leader, earning personal credibility and creating an emotional connection between yourself and your audience is essential if you want to succeed. Don't just rely on logic. Storytelling is one of the most effective ways to ensure you include a focus on both ethos and pathos.

We see Aristotle's model of influence as a three-legged stool. Right now most of us are trying to sit on stools that have one really long leg (logic) and two barely-there legs (personal credibility and emotional connection). So let's try to even out those legs. Combining logic, personal credibility and emotional connection when you communicate will dramatically increase your chances of becoming an inspiring leader.

We are assuming you need no help with logos — you probably have all the logic you need to present your messages. What we do ask you to consider is how you can establish both ethos and pathos within your messages.

Let's look at a couple of examples of when logos, ethos and pathos have been used together to achieve staggering success.

One very public example of the Aristotle model being used to influence is the 2006 documentary film *The Inconvenient Truth*, based on former US Vice President Al Gore's slide show about climate change and global warming. The data and the logic around climate change and global warming was already well known. However, Al Gore was one of the first people to bring personal credibility and emotional connection to the table. His passion and interest in climate change was well documented and he was the first person to create an emotional connection to the issue by showing polar bears losing their habitat. It is an excellent example of all three components of Aristotle's model working together.

Loredana Moretto, a leadership development consultant, faced the challenge of connecting with her audience in a credible and emotional way. She was responsible for recruiting emerging leaders into a year-long leadership-development program. While the process was transparent and provided all the logos people needed, she wanted to show her audience that she had a real commitment to keeping it transparent and providing both the successful and the unsuccessful candidates with feedback. This is the story she used to tap into ethos and pathos.

Crusty Mrs Ford

As a little girl in primary school, I loved school. I grew up in South Africa and the school system there was such that we had a new teacher every year. And every year I was blessed with teachers who liked me. I was an athlete and I loved my school work.

One year I had a teacher named Mrs Ford, or as I came to nickname her, 'crusty' Mrs Ford.

Mrs Ford, for reasons I could not understand, treated me differently from the other children. I was never invited to take part in the 'cool' projects at school. I was excluded, but I never knew why. I tried really, really hard to improve my school work, but to no avail.

One day there was a kerfuffle in the front row of the class. I was in that front row, but what had happened was not my fault. She looked up and, without even asking what had happened, she singled me out and told me to sit on the floor in front of the whole class to do my schoolwork. You cannot imagine my humiliation. There I was on the floor, like an animal, in front of my little classmates. From that day onwards I became disengaged and disinterested at school.

Fortunately, my next teacher was terrific and I got back on track. I always got feedback. I knew what was happening and why, and how it affected me.

But why am I sharing my 'Crusty Mrs Ford' experience with you? Today I am responsible for running leadership development programs. My experience has taught me that no-one who applies to get into the program — whether they are successful or not — will ever, on my watch, have the 'Crusty Mrs Ford' experience.

It is really important to understand how much a story can help with both credibility and emotional engagement. Stories are perhaps the most efficient and effective way to include these two essential forms of influence when you are attempting to connect, engage and inspire people.

The curse of knowledge

Leaders who use stories intuitively agree that it is their obligation to communicate their message in a way that their audience will understand it.

> *Respect your audience. It's not their job to 'get it'; it's your job to communicate it to them.*

> **Brian McDonald, author of *Invisible Ink: A Practical Guide to Building Stories that Resonate***

These leaders understand that by default everyone has the curse of knowledge. The trick is to find ways of avoiding the curse. So what is the curse of knowledge? We first came across the term 'curse of knowledge' while we were reading about research conducted by Elizabeth Newton for her PhD at Stanford University.

Newton conducted a simple experiment in which she asked a group of volunteers to pair off. One person in each pair was given the role of 'tapper' and the other the role of 'listener'. Each tapper received a list of 25 well-known songs such as 'Happy Birthday' and a list of nursery rhymes. The tappers had to choose a song and tap it out to the listeners, who had to try to guess the title of the song. Simple.

Newton asked the tappers what they thought their success rate would be and they estimated that 50 per cent of the time the listeners would guess the song. The actual result was a surprisingly low 2.5 per cent. Why do you think that was? It was because of the curse of knowledge. Once the tappers had the song title firmly implanted in their minds, they could not imagine what it was like not knowing it. Their knowledge (the song title) had cursed them.

Newton stated that these results demonstrate that we over-estimate our ability as communicators. We are also cursed by the knowledge that we have because we expect others to have the same knowledge. We think that once we have told people something they will 'get it'. (Anyone with children will testify that this is not the case!)

The curse of knowledge is something no-one wants,
but — unfortunately — everyone has.

Like a dreaded disease, anyone can be struck down by the curse of knowledge at any time. When leaders communicate a strategy or a major change, they are often hit with the curse of knowledge. They have been talking about the strategy for days, weeks or often months and then expect people to understand it in a one-hour presentation.

You will be affected by the curse of knowledge in many areas of your life. We all are. Think about the last presentation you delivered. Did you suffer from the curse of knowledge? What about when you talk to clients or present to your team? Think about what you say. Ask yourself if you are potentially cursed by your knowledge.

So the first step is to understand that by default you will have the curse of knowledge. Now we can get on with showing you how to avoid it.

Avoiding the curse

As Denzel Washington says in the movie *Philadelphia*, 'Explain it to me like I'm a four-year-old'. This is a great line and a great way to dodge the curse of knowledge. In a nutshell, run whatever it is you're trying to communicate past someone who knows absolutely nothing about it. You don't need to dumb things down and you don't need to be condescending, but would a kid understand what you are saying?

One of the other very successful ways to dodge the curse of knowledge is to use a story.

Successful business storytellers make the complex, simple without dumbing down the information. In the 1960s, John F. Kennedy (J.F.K) had a vision: space travel. At this time, the average Joe hadn't even been on an aircraft. So how did J.F.K sell his vision to the masses? By saying, 'We are going to put a man on the moon and bring him safely back to earth by the end of the decade'.

In *Made to Stick* Dan and Chip Heath write that if J.F.K had been a modern-day CEO he would probably have said something along the lines of, 'Our mission is to become the international leader in the space industry through maximum team-centred innovation and strategically targeted aerospace initiatives'. Yikes!

Urban legend has it that when J.F.K was visiting NASA he met a cleaner. J.F.K asked him, 'What do you do?' The cleaner replied, 'I'm helping to put a man on the moon'.

Imagine if your messages had that much cut-through. Imagine if everyone in your company — from your senior leadership team to your front-line and back-end employees — had that amount of clarity on the strategic direction of the company. As a leader, you should be aiming at that same level of clarity, understanding and engagement. You can only do that if your messages are relevant, engaging and meaningful.

One of our clients is the chief information officer (CIO) of a global finance company. Her latest employee opinion survey showed that the employee engagement scores were spiralling out of control and she did not know why. We did some consulting work, which included conducting focus groups with the employees to ascertain their understanding of the company's new strategy.

We then met with the CIO to share the results with her. When we mentioned the employees' lack of understanding around the strategy, she physically hit the desk in frustration and said, 'I can't believe this. The vision and strategy has been communicated so many times and the diagram of it is on every piece of communication'. She then showed us the latest PowerPoint presentation and pointed to the corner. In the corner was a diagram of the strategy. The diagram was a professional image and it looked quite effective, but it was very, very 'busy'. We responded with, 'Oh, that must be the "spaceship" everyone talked about'.

We genuinely felt her pain because she thought she was doing everything right. In business she may have thought a designed graphic image represented a new strategy correctly. In reality the diagram was over-complicated. Without some stories to help make sense of the strategy, no-one would understand it or relate to it. This CIO and her leadership team were suffering from the curse of knowledge. In their minds they had communicated the strategy — and had communicated it many times — via this diagram. However, no-one understood it, and the leaders became frustrated because of their wasted efforts. Meanwhile employee engagement scores were heading south.

The leaders were then introduced to the concept of storytelling and how it could help them dodge the curse of knowledge.

They started using stories to communicate the strategy, which resulted in a 9-per-cent increase in their employee engagement scores.

> *Communicating complex messages in a way people understand is really hard. Using jargon is easy. It is not until you truly understand something that you can communicate it in a way everyone else understands.*

John Stewart, Chairman, Legal and General, London and Director, Telstra Corporation, Melbourne

During the Global Financial Crisis in 2008, when John Stewart was CEO of National Australia Bank, the bank literally had to change its strategy overnight. John, who was an avid sailor and had competed several times in the Sydney to Hobart Yacht Race, communicated the importance of changing strategy via a story about sailing. He recalled his sailing experiences when the conditions become dangerous and would say to his employees that the focus shifts from winning the race to ensuring that the boat and the crew get through the storm unscathed.

This story filtered down throughout the organisation as leader after leader repeated it to their own team. When this happens you know you have, as a leader, dodged the curse of knowledge. This story also helped John Stewart deliver on the three challenges of leadership communication: knowing the audience understands what you are saying, can remember what you said and can recall it.

A few years later, John shared with us that he communicated the need for an entire organisational change in strategic direction through that one simple story ... and it worked.

As a leader in business you may want to think carefully about where you potentially have the curse of knowledge and consider how storytelling can help you dodge that curse of knowledge.

In a nutshell

Did you get hooked?

→ Only dinosaurs stick with the facts.

→ The role of the leader as purely an information provider is extinct.

→ You are a leader, not Google, so you cannot simply deliver the facts and data. You have to provide information in a way that is relevant, engaging and meaningful.

→ Facts and data are hard to remember. You cannot get people hooked on just the facts.

→ To connect, engage and inspire as a leader you have to understand and embrace the fact that emotions help people remember, help to trigger action and that they are the fast track to the brain.

→ Storytelling is the simplest yet most effective way to tap into emotions.

→ In addition to the facts, logic and emotion, as a leader you need credibility and people have to trust you before they will trust your message.

→ Aristotle's model of influence demonstrates that we need logic, personal credibility and emotional connection to successfully persuade, and that storytelling can help us do this.

→ We all have the curse of knowledge. Beware of this and dodge it by using storytelling.

How hooked are you?

→ Review your current methods of communication using the Aristotle model: from the way you conduct team meetings, to your presentations, to your written emails. How much of it falls into the logic space compared to the ethos and pathos spaces?

→ Identify where you could possibly have the curse of knowledge. Is it a phrase you always use, or is it related to a new strategy? Think back over the past month: do you remember saying or thinking, 'Why don't they get it?' That is always a good indication that you may have the curse of knowledge.

In this chapter we explored why leaders need storytelling, why specifically storytelling and why now. The next chapter will help you identify what kind of business storyteller you are.

CHAPTER 3

Business storytelling styles

There's always room for a story that can transport people to another place.

J.K. Rowling, author

The good news is that everyone has the ability to tell stories — including stories with a strong purpose that are gripping and enjoyable and that influence action. The first thing you need is to identify the type of storyteller you are. That way you will be able to work on the areas you need to address or improve on. That's what we will be looking at in this chapter.

Then, in chapter 4, we will get into the juicy stuff of crafting your stories.

The four types of storyteller

In the years of running our workshops, we have observed many different leaders across a variety of businesses and industries. Regardless of position, age, gender or race, we have noticed that there are four distinct styles of business storyteller:

- The Avoider (low engagement and low purpose)
- The Joker (high engagement and low purpose)

- The Reporter (low engagement and high purpose)
- The Inspirer (high engagement and high purpose).

Each style is determined by two factors.

The first measures how engaging your story is. This ranges from a very low or complete lack of engagement, where you have failed to get the listener's attention or interest, to a really high level of engagement, where the listener is hooked on every word you say.

The second factor determines whether your story has a strong purpose. This again will range from low, where you are not sure why you are telling the story or what you want the story to achieve, to high, where your purpose is crystal clear and you know what you want your audience to think, feel and, most importantly, *do* differently after they have heard the story.

To help you determine your business storytelling style, we developed the Dolan Naidu Story Intelligence Model shown in figure 3.1.

The purpose of this model is to indicate the four storytelling styles and to help you identify your style. Once you know your style you can be aware of the aspects of storytelling you need to specifically focus on to move to the Inspire quadrant.

Let's now explore the four storytelling styles.

Figure 3.1: the Dolan Naidu Story Intelligence Model

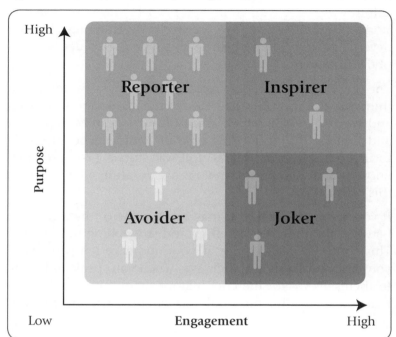

The Avoider

Avoiders come in many guises. If you are an Avoider, you may avoid using stories altogether! It is likely you think it's inappropriate to use stories in business, based on what you have learned in the past and the various organisations and cultures you have worked in. You probably don't believe that storytelling will work. You are probably thinking, 'I could never tell a story'. In a nutshell, this type of Avoider is afraid of the unknown.

The other type of Avoider actually uses stories — at least, you think you do. Your so-called 'stories' tend to be about yourself and your successes, which — put bluntly — can be repetitive and lifeless. If you are this type of Avoider, you probably focus on 'the good old days' and war stories. (You probably know at least one person in your organisation who falls into this category!)

If you are an Avoider, you may be unaware of the difference between traditional storytelling and storytelling in business. This comes at a high price as your audience tends to avoid you! They probably roll their eyes when you speak and think to themselves, 'Not the cricket story again'. Thankfully, now that you are reading this book this will no longer be the case!

The Joker

If you are a Joker...you guessed it: you tell lots of funny stories. Chances are you get invited out to the pub a lot. You are the life and soul of the party! Other people love hearing your stories. Your main purpose is to get people to laugh, which is an admirable quality to have. However, although your stories are really engaging, they rarely have a purpose except to make people laugh. Therefore, you are missing out on a lot of business opportunities!

Once you learn to nail the purpose of your story — what you want it to achieve from a business point of view — it will have much greater impact. You already narrate engaging and memorable stories, so imagine the impact you would have if your stories were directly related to a business objective.

The Reporter

The Reporter is by far the most common style in business. Almost 90 per cent of business people operate in this style. If you are a Reporter, you use lots of facts, figures, statistics, case studies, business examples and any other data you can get your hands on.

Reporting will feel like your natural style even though this is not a natural style, but a learnt style. It is something you have learned over time. In business, we have been educated over the past couple of decades that 'business is business. It is all about the facts and figures. There is no room for emotion in business'. So it's no wonder that many people's stories in business tend to be about reporting the details.

While Reporters usually have a clear purpose, they are low on engagement; people simply don't connect with them. You know what you want your audience to feel or act on but, unfortunately, your PowerPoint slides and statistics are putting them into a coma! Learning to bring in emotion using storytelling will remedy that.

The Inspirer

If you are an Inspirer you have a clear purpose for each and every story you tell. You are not afraid to share personal stories, or to show your vulnerability and open yourself up to people. Your audience, therefore, engages with you. They listen to you with bated breath. You know exactly how to connect a personal story with a business message.

As you will come to realise while reading this book, personal stories are often about quite mundane, everyday things such as walking the dog or visiting your local hardware store. Paradoxically, that is where the power is because people relate to the ordinary and see parallels in their own life. Hence, an

Inspirer does not need to be a world-renowned mountaineer with one leg.

Inspirers have a variety of stories that they prepare, practise and continue to add to. You remember and connect when you hear an Inspirer's story. Think back to some of the most inspiring leaders you know, the most inspiring teacher you had or the most inspiring presenter you have seen. We can almost guarantee that what inspired you was one of two things: the actions and decisions they made or the stories they shared. Being an inspiring storyteller is where you should aim to be.

Now we want to make it clear what we mean by Inspirer. We would hate you to think that you have to turn into Martin Luther King. Nor are we suggesting you need to be a chest-pumping, fist-in-the-air person whipping your audience into a frenzy. When we say 'Inspirer' we mean that you have to be able to connect with your audience and influence them to action … and you can do that authentically and within your own natural style.

Let's now look at an example of how one leader became an inspiring storyteller. Jeff had an ongoing issue with his team members, who refused to take initiatives and expected management to solve all the problems. He had previously shared stories about the importance of taking initiatives, but his stories were very much told in the Reporter style.

This is a story he developed during one of our workshops.

The microwave story

A few years ago I was the country manager for Iran and we had an issue with our lunchroom. There was only one microwave, which meant at lunchtime there was a long queue of people waiting to heat up their lunch and they could not sit and eat together. Management's great solution? Buy a second microwave! This did help for a while. The queues were shorter and two people could sit and eat at a time.

One day our long-serving cleaner, Fatemah, said that if we purchased a cooking pot, she would be happy to prepare fresh rice each day to help out. The team loved this because not only did it save them from heating up their rice in the microwave, it was also fresh.

The next week, Fatemah gave out hand-written menus, offering to cook a different dish each day for a fair price. Fatemah transformed our lunchtimes. The lunchroom became a happy place where we sat and ate good food together and shared stories.

By her own initiative, Fatemah changed herself from cleaner to cook, increasing her income and proving management do not have all the solutions.

How many of us are like Fatemah, with ideas and initiatives inside us just waiting to be let loose?

When Jeff shared this story during his team meetings and one on one with people in his team, he noticed more and more people taking initiatives when challenges and opportunities presented themselves.

Determining your style

It is time to answer a question honestly: where do you currently place yourself on the Dolan Naidu Story Intelligence Model?

It is possible that you move between the styles in the model according to different situations, but this may be more by accident than through deliberate design. In your personal life you may be a Joker, whereas in business you may be an Avoider. You will, however, have a default style that you feel most comfortable with. As we said, most people in business are Reporters, but even if you place yourself in that category today, this does not mean it has to be your category tomorrow.

By the end of this book, with a bit of practice of course, you will be telling inspiring stories that are engaging and have a clear purpose — you will be an inspiring business storyteller.

If you honestly feel that you are already an inspiring storyteller, first of all, make sure you are not an Avoider in disguise! Conduct a reality check with those around you, asking them what style they think you are. You may be surprised. If you get the green light from everyone, then good for you! There is still much more to learn though, so stay tuned.

It starts with you

Just as Michael Jackson sings in his song 'Man in the Mirror', for any change to take place in your business, you have to first look at yourself.

You must be the change you want to see in the world.

**Mahatma Gandhi, father of India's
independence movement**

Now that you know what type of storyteller you are, we need to set you up on the road to becoming a totally inspiring storyteller so that you can begin crafting stories.

A moment of truth first: this is not a model such as Myers-Briggs where it is perfectly okay to be anywhere on the model. In this model you are absolutely aiming for the top, right-hand quadrant: the Inspirer.

Here are some specific areas you should focus on to make sure you move into the zone of the Inspirer.

Focus areas

No matter which style of storyteller you currently consider yourself to be, the following tips will help you become a true Inspirer.

The Avoider

- Start small but start somewhere. Get over your fear of telling stories.
- Observe other storytellers: learn what they do well and what they do not.
- Include only relevant detail in your stories — that means having a very clear purpose.
- Retire stories that you have been using for years, or give them an overhaul.

The Joker

- Avoid using humour purely for the sake of it.
- Make sure humour adds to the purpose of the story rather than distracting from it.

- Ensure you have some stories without humour.

- Seek feedback from trusted friends and mentors to ensure your style is not negatively impacting on your career and personal brand. (This could be a tough conversation, but it can be life changing.)

The Reporter

- Do not just use case studies and business examples — consider how you can use personal stories in addition to these.

- Do not be afraid to use a story for even the most serious and complex messages. They are the ones that perhaps warrant a story the most.

- Separate your story out from the facts and figures. So, avoid including statistics, percentages and facts in your stories as they will then start to move from story to case study.

The Inspirer

- Ensure you have a variety of stories and that you keep replenishing your stories.

- Master the skill of listening to other people's stories to take your storytelling to the next level.

- Be ruthless. There is a fine line between being inspiring and being self-indulgent. Strip out anything you enjoy telling that really does not add to the story or its purpose.

- Beware of becoming complacent with your storytelling. Keep on practising, polishing and refining.

Storytelling is a skill that can be taught and learnt. The Dolan Naidu Story Intelligence Model will help you determine where you are at and this book will give you the tools to move into the Inspirer quadrant.

In a nutshell

Did you get hooked?

→ There are four storytelling styles:

1 Avoider (low engagement and low purpose)

2 Joker (high engagement and low purpose)

3 Reporter (low engagement and high purpose)

4 Inspirer (high engagement and high purpose).

→ The Inspirer is what you want to be.

→ Be prepared to change yourself first and become the role model in your company.

How hooked are you?

Do an honest assessment of where you are on the Dolan Naidu Story Intelligence Model and review your areas for improvement.

Now you should know what type of storyteller you are. In the next chapter we will help you to start crafting your stories.

CHAPTER 4

Crafting your stories

What really counts is that I am Irish and I know how to tell a story.

Jack Welch, American business executive and author, when asked about his most important attribute

Rosemary Reed was a risk adviser with a large global company. One of the key challenges Rosemary faced was explaining to her colleagues in the business that the role of the risk adviser was not to manage risks for the business, but to provide them with the knowledge and advice to manage their own risk. They, however, thought it was her role to manage risk. She tried to tell them several times that this was not the case, but the message did not get through. This is the story she came up with to make them understand and remember.

The copperhead snake

I grew up in the country and can always remember my mum telling me about the dangers and risks around our property: from red-back spiders, to the dangers of the creek and the snakes in summer. She always used to say, 'When you come across these risks you need to know what to do because I will not always be there'.

(continued)

The copperhead snake (cont'd)

One stinking hot day, Mum kept telling me to go and get my bike, which I had left at the bottom of the garden path. I remember reluctantly running down the path to get it and just as I got close I noticed a huge copperhead snake curled up in front of my bike, basking in the sun.

I slid to a stop and froze … my first reaction was to go running and screaming back to the house to tell Mum. But I didn't … I played statues and, without taking my eyes off the snake, I very slowly walked backwards. I did exactly what my mum had previously told me to do. When there was enough distance between me and the snake I turned around and ran back to the house, screaming.

I often think about what my mum did for me and the role we have as risk advisers. Mum gave me advice and skills so I would have the confidence and knowledge to know what to do.

In risk management we play a similar role. We can't own and manage the risks when they arise. Our aim is to give you — the business — sufficient knowledge and tools so that when you come across your own copperhead snake — regardless of what it looks like — you will know what to do.

Rosemary's story helped her achieve the change she needed. On hearing this story, her audience immediately understood her role and how it was their responsibility, not Rosemary's, to manage risk.

In this chapter we are going to show you how you can craft a motivating story like Rosemary's — a story that will help you connect with your audience and inspire action.

Establish your purpose

In previous chapters we discussed when and why you use stories in business. To recap: stories influence, persuade, connect and engage. Each and every story you craft must be authentic, be supported by data and have a very clear and specific purpose. Whether it is to get your employees to increase their productivity, or to sell a new product to a client, first of all you have to identify what action you want your audience to take. In other words, you have to establish the purpose of your story. By 'purpose' we mean the single message your story conveys.

Great minds have purposes, others have wishes.

Washington Irving, author

Clarifying your purpose is not easy. Some people start this process with 'I want to change the sales culture', or 'I want my team to get excited about the new strategy'. These are very broad statements. The reality is that you will need lots of stories to change a sales culture and you will need lots of stories to get all your employees excited about a strategy. So the key is to break your big-picture purpose down into lots of specific purposes and come up with a few different stories with very different, specific purposes.

The two steps to take are:

1 *Ask yourself the following question:* What is the one key message I want my audience to take away with them? (One message = one story.)

2 *Convert your answer into a bumper sticker:* stick it on everything from your car to your cupboard doors. This will help you sum up the essence of your story.

So if your message is, 'Innovation involves hard work and risking failure' you may end up with lots of bumper stickers such as, 'Just do it', 'Better to have tried and failed than not to have tried at all' and '99 per cent perspiration, 1 per cent inspiration' and each of these would merit a story.

Getting your purpose right

There are some common mistakes people make when determining their purpose. Let's look at these so you can avoid them.

There must be a purpose

You would be surprised how many people do not actually have a purpose for their stories. They tell a story, but are not sure or clear on the message they want to convey through the story. While this is okay in your personal life, it defeats the point of using stories in business.

Don't try to solve world hunger with one story

Don't try to achieve the impossible with your story. Clients often tell us that they want to communicate the story of their brand or strategy — that's like trying to solve world hunger with one story. Your brand story is best told as many stories, each with a different purpose. One purpose could be to show that your brand is innovative, another that it has integrity or prides itself on service.

People usually start with a purpose that is too large. By using the two steps above you can crystallise your single purpose. As you break your *big* purpose into lots of smaller purposes each of them will merit a story. Remember the brussels sprouts story and Michael Brandt's purpose of meeting sales targets (see p. 3)? Initially Michael's purpose was to change the sales culture. That is too big a purpose for one story. Changing a sales culture requires lots of stories. The brussels sprouts story was only one of them.

Avoid jargon

Jargon is big business. Business is absolutely full of it, from 'optimising synergies', to 'executional excellence', to 'step change'. Here is the reality: most people do not know what those catchcries mean and other people have different understandings of what they mean. Jargon is abstract so it just bounces off people's heads.

When it comes to your purpose, you need to break down every word into simple, everyday language. So if your purpose includes 'optimised synergies', think about what you really mean by that. Do you want your team to work together — for them to feel like they have made a contribution? Think about your purpose in everyday words people can relate to and reword your purpose accordingly.

Don't have too many purposes

'I want people to understand our new strategy, be passionate about it, explain it to their teams so their teams connect with it and articulate it convincingly to our clients and stakeholders.'

Get it? No, we don't either. The statement contains three different purposes rolled into one. Let's break it down:

- 'I want everyone to understand our new strategy and be passionate about it.'

- 'I want our team leaders to explain the new strategy to their teams so they connect with it and articulate it.'

- 'I want our new strategy to be articulated to our clients and stakeholders in a way that will make them feel excited by it.'

Trying to tackle lots of issues in one hit will supersize your story and take away from the story's impact and effectiveness. It can also leave people feeling baffled and thinking, 'What was that all about?'

You must believe in your purpose

In addition, as the storyteller you need to believe in your story and its purpose. Your intent has to be authentic.

A few years ago we did some work with a leadership team that was outsourcing some of its work overseas and looking for stories to communicate this. When no stories emerged we asked them, 'Can you honestly put your hand on your heart and say you believe this is the best thing for your company?' They couldn't. Unless you believe in the purpose you are not going to have an authentic story. We advised the leadership team to just go with the data, which they did.

At this point you may want to have a think about your story's purpose or purposes. You may even want to write it down and as step 2 of that, convert it into a bumper sticker.

Establish who you're talking to

Any form of communication, including storytelling, must have a clear audience. Storytelling without an audience in mind is like 'storytelling in the dark' — it is downright dangerous. Winging it really is for amateurs. And you are not an amateur. Business storytelling is only successful when you shine a light on your audience.

You have to research your audience inside and out. Who are they? What motivates them? What do they fear or get excited by?

If you do not know your audience very well, speak to someone who knows them better than you do. Research your audience as much as possible.

Inspiring storytellers start by understanding how their audience thinks, feels and acts.

I made mistakes in drama. I thought drama was when actors cried. But drama is when the audience cries.

Frank Capra, film director

There are three questions you must ask yourself before you begin crafting your story:

- Who is your audience?
- What motivates your audience? (What makes them tick?)
- What are your audience's concerns?

Let's have a look at each of these.

Who is your audience?

Carolyn Tate, a marketing guru and friend, once asked a financial planner who his audience was and he replied, 'Anybody with a pulse really'. The last thing we ever want to hear you say is that your stories are for everybody…with a pulse. That is one way of guaranteeing your stories will fail.

So what are you presenting or writing and who is going to listen to or read it? Is it your direct team, the venture capitalists to whom you are pitching or the salespeople in your company? The more narrowly you define your audience, the more successful you are going to be as a storyteller. Even if your story may be relevant to everyone in your organisation, initially you should pick an audience segment for your story and construct the story around that audience segment.

What motivates your audience?

Remember Michael Brandt, who hated brussels sprouts but was able to use them to inspire his sales teams to meet their monthly targets (see p. 3)?

Michael lived, breathed and worked hard for sales leads. He knew they were the fuel of his business and that success depended on them. Converting leads into new customers and new business was something he was very proud of and passionate about doing. But his audience did not think the same way as he did.

It turned out his teams despised sales leads. They found them difficult to generate and less than enjoyable to work on, so most of his team put them off until the very last minute on a Friday afternoon. Consequently, a lot of leads were missed as his team rushed out the door for the weekend — and the sales targets suffered as a result.

Notice how Michael's perspective differs from that of his team? Imagine if Michael had not actually taken the time to put himself in his audience's shoes. Imagine if he had crafted a story that talked about the importance of sales leads instead of addressing what was important to his audience. A story on the importance of sales leads would have had no impact or, even worse, a negative impact.

Remember, you may want your employees to love every aspect of their job just as you may want your customers to love every single product and service you have, but that is not reality!

What are your audience's concerns?

What concerns does your audience have? What worries them? What do they fear? Are they threatened by the high frequency of change in your company or the quality of one of the products they have to sell? Or the consequence if they fail to meet their KPIs? Unless you take the time to find out and address these issues, your story will lack empathy and come across as fake and unauthentic.

One of our clients, Liza Boston, is a successful, energetic entrepreneur in the social media space. She had to sell her services to large organisations when social media was a relatively new concept — not an easy thing to do. She initially thought it was because they did not understand the opportunities that social media could bring them.

After helping Liza analyse her audience, we discovered the real issue was fear. The people Liza was trying to connect with feared taking a risk and failing.

Liza told us that after she had finished taking one potential client through the benefits of her proposal she could still feel a reluctance to proceed. So, although she was a bit tentative herself about telling a story to a group of people, she thought she may as well give it a go. This is the story she told them.

Mount Hutt

A few years ago I went skiing with a friend on Mount Hutt in New Zealand. One night it snowed heavily and we awoke to a perfect day of skiing. Yet half of the mountain was closed while safety checks and potential avalanche tests were conducted. We would catch the chairlift up to the summit and to our right we could see the perfect snow that was out of bounds.

One time while on the chairlift, we had two instructors in front of us and when they arrived at the summit, instead of going down the side of the mountain that everyone was going down they skied over to the other side and turned the 'closed' sign to 'open'. We immediately followed them. We were unbelievably

(continued)

> **Mount Hutt (cont'd)**
>
> excited, but really anxious because we were taking the risk of being the first to ski down that side of the mountain. After a slight hesitation, we took a leap of faith and screamed with delight as we followed the instructors down.
>
> I feel like we are on the summit with you and there is a whole side of the mountain we can help you explore. Like those ski instructors we will be your guides, helping you avoid all the risks while enjoying all the benefits.

One woman had sat through the whole meeting with her arms crossed, looking disengaged. As soon as Liza started telling the story, the woman unfolded her arms and leaned forward in her chair and her entire body language changed. For the first time in that meeting she smiled. After listening to the story, the group started talking among themselves about how they could get this through the risk department and how they could get funding.

Let's look at another example from the advertising world that illustrates the importance of knowing who your audience is, what motivates them and what their concerns are.

In November 2012, Metro Trains Melbourne released a campaign to raise awareness of safety at train stations. Too many people, especially young people, were being killed or badly injured by trains at stations. With every death or close call, spokespeople from the train companies, the police and politicians gave the public very logical reasons why acting in an unsafe manner near fast-moving trains is dangerous.

Metro's safety campaign is titled 'Dumb Ways To Die' and consists of a three-minute song and video clip. The clip uses black comedy and features a range of cute little bean characters being killed doing really dumb things. The final three characters are killed by trains due to poor safety at train stations.

The clip was loaded onto YouTube on 14 November 2012. It went viral and became an internet sensation. Within 20 days of hitting YouTube it attracted more than 30 million views and more than 300 parodies. The accompanying song was also released on iTunes and within 24 hours was in the top 10 on the iTunes chart in Australia. It also reached the top 10 on iTunes charts in Hong Kong, Singapore, Taiwan and Vietnam. To find the clip, search YouTube for 'Dumb Ways to Die'.

When you watch the three-minute clip or read the lyrics, you will notice that it is not until the two-minute and 20-second mark that the message about train safety kicks in. The makers spent 75 per cent of their time building a connection with their audience before delivering their message. They also identified perfectly the key emotion their audience would relate to. The target audience for the message is young adults and children. So while you may initially think they are appealing to their audience by using a catchy song, at a deeper level they have tapped into the right emotion for their audience. Kids — especially young adults — think they are bulletproof.

The message that 'poor safety around trains could lead to your death' would have had little impact. But the message that 'poor safety around trains means you are dumb' has impact. They are not so worried about death, but looking dumb is a major concern for this audience.

With your purpose in mind, have a think about your audience, identifying who they are, what motivates them and what their concerns are. Once you have your purpose and audience, you can then start looking for stories you can use.

Where do stories come from?

'Oh, I don't have any stories,' you may be thinking to yourself, or 'I don't have any interesting stories'. Wrong! Life is rich with stories.

You can create your stories from either business or personal experiences.

Business stories

Business stories are stories about events that happen in business — either something you have experienced in your career, or a story about another leader, a customer or a project you worked on. These stories tend to be literal: if you are looking for a story on selling you would go and speak to a salesperson; if you are looking for leadership stories you would speak to other leaders.

This can work, especially in sales and long-term organisational change. What you need to be careful of with business stories, however, is that they do not turn into case studies. It is also harder to tap into emotion using business stories.

Business stories have a tendency to stay in the 'logic' space. You can avoid this trap — but it is important to know that there is a potential trap with business stories.

One way of finding business stories is to tap into your business experiences in either your current or a previous role. You may also read something or hear something about another business that you could use. For example, you may have read the *Smart Company* article on the five best Steve Jobs anecdotes and share what you read, as in the following story.

> ## Business story ideas
>
> I was recently reading a *Smart Company* article on Steve Jobs. Jobs was shown a prototype of the iPad and complained that it was too big. When the engineers told him they couldn't make it any smaller, Jobs took it over to an aquarium and dropped it into the water.
>
> 'These are air bubbles,' he said. 'That means there's space in there. Make it smaller'. Reading the article reminded me of the opportunity we have here at work. Even though we do great work, there is always opportunity for improvement.

Another good way of finding interesting business stories is to start asking questions. You do not have to carry out a full-on interview with your customers or employees, but when, for example, a customer gives you good feedback, ask them some key follow-up questions such as 'How exactly did it help you?'. Dig deep and you will be surprised what stories you will uncover. You can then use your customers' experiences as your stories. This method is simple and gives good results, but it is sadly underused.

Personal stories

Personal stories draw from your everyday personal life. This is where you can use everyday personal experiences and link them to a business message. If you look at the many stories we have already shared, all of them have been personal. Remember the Bruce Springsteen story and Crusty Mrs Ford? Done right, personal stories are extremely refreshing to hear in business.

Personal stories are lateral stories, meaning they take two things that seem completely unrelated (think brussels sprouts and sales leads) and connect them in a way that makes perfect sense.

From doing the gardening on the weekend, to watching a movie or your days at university, personal experiences are the best basis for stories simply because everyone can relate to personal stories, whether they are about dropping kids off at school, catching a flight or renovating your house.

Stories about your own children are great because they show your audience your human side and they are something many people can relate to. This is why it is important that you understand your audience well. For example, if you are going to be presenting to a group of mothers of teenage children, then a story about teaching your kids to drive will be a sure-fire hit.

Personal stories are refreshing and universally appealing.

Candice Lance used her personal experience to craft this story. Her audience was her leadership team and her purpose was to communicate that sometimes it is okay to let go and trust the experts.

It's okay to let go

The plane had just reached 3600 metres. I was sitting on the edge of the open door. The time had come: it was my turn. In just a split second my mind raced: What was I thinking? What did I have to do? What did they tell me? Was the guy behind me having a good day? Was this really a good idea?

It didn't really matter what the answer was to any of those questions — I was out the door. No turning back. I was bending like a banana, holding on like I was told, remembering my training and plummeting towards the ground — I was tandem sky diving!

What a rush. I was flying. I was free. As we continued to fall I remembered the videos of this moment as people landed safely on the ground crying and hugging their instructor and I thought, 'What saps, I would never do that'. Moments later my feet touched the ground and I was jumping up and down, hugging my instructor … and crying — yes what a sap!

I am not sure if I would go sky diving again, but I did learn a lesson or two. Sometimes it is okay to let go; sometimes it is okay to be out of control. And it is definitely okay to trust your training and the people who are the trained experts.

Our clients often tell us that this is the biggest lesson they have had: how to use personal stories in a work context. Your challenge is linking those personal stories to the purpose of your story. And the purpose of your story will always be business related. This is a very important distinction and it separates the inspiring storyteller from the rest.

One of our clients, Louise, was due to present to her team about their communication methods. She wanted them to spend more time proofreading their outgoing emails as many were being sent with spelling mistakes and incorrect data. The company was wasting a lot of precious hours and money fixing up these mistakes.

She crafted this story to tell them.

Tissues in the wash

Last month, after a busy day at work, I rushed home to cook dinner and attend to a dozen chores that are part of everyday family life. I also decided to put on a load of washing. I was pleased with how many things I was ticking off my list — and so speedily too. When I went to get the washing out, I was horrified to find it covered with white tissue shreds. In my rush, I had forgotten to check the pockets for tissues and my son's pants had had a whole packet of tissues stuffed in them. I was really angry with him and cursed him for the next hour or so as I tried to remove all the tissue pieces from every piece of clothing. Once I had calmed down I realised if I had only taken a couple of minutes to check the pockets before hitting the start button it would have saved me hours of wasted time spent going over all the clothes with a lint brush. I would rather check for tissues in pockets (which takes two minutes) than work for hours on the after-effects.

When you think about our communication at work, imagine the difference we could make if we checked for 'tissues' in our emails before hitting the send button.

So, yes, you can even find your next story in your washing machine! There's almost a limitless ocean of stories out there once you embrace the opportunity that personal stories bring.

Notice that we said *almost* a limitless ocean — so is anything off limits when sharing personal experiences? The answer is 'yes'.

It is not a good idea to use personal experiences that include sex, religion or politics. We would also advise you to be careful when sharing personal tragedies as this may be uncomfortable for your audience and uncomfortable for you. Successful storytelling, especially where you use personal experiences as the basis of your stories, is about self-disclosure. But only you as the storyteller can determine the level of self-disclosure that is right for your purpose, for your audience and for you. Trust yourself and if you are unsure ask someone you trust for their opinion.

Please also steer clear of any 'how great I am' stories. Unless they are told with the right level of humility and self-deprecation, these stories can backfire and be a complete turn-off for your audience. As a leader it is worth noting that praise is great as long as it is not about you, so the one thing that is categorically off limits is only sharing experiences that show how great you are!

What about negative experiences (stories around failure) that present you as the leader in a less than flattering light? Stories about failure absolutely work—in fact we encourage you to share these 'life-is-less-than-perfect' stories. As a leader, sharing your failures is a sign of strength. It helps people connect with you as it humanises you.

Here's an example of a leader, Oshana De Silva, who shared a story around her blind spot and used it to create a powerful learning experience for all the leaders in the room.

Girls don't like dinosaurs

My daughter, who is four, was preparing for 'Show and tell' in her new kinder class. She decided to take her favourite dinosaur, Sophie, to school and we planned what she would say and even practised it. She was very excited.

The day arrived and she carefully took Sophie to kinder, the occasion marked by a pink bow around Sophie's neck. That afternoon, after kinder, I asked her how she went. She was

(continued)

> ## Girls don't like dinosaurs (cont'd)
>
> very low key about it and then she blurted out, 'Mummy, my friends said girls don't like dinosaurs'. My heart fell to my boots. I didn't know then that these words would come back to haunt me.
>
> A week or so later I attended a business breakfast where I was presented with some statistics. They said that 41 per cent of men wanted workplace flexibility. I had a big 'a-ha' moment. I realised I had spoken to all my female team members about workplace flexibility, but never to any of my male team members. I had my own grown-up version of 'Girls don't like dinosaurs'. It was, 'Men don't want flexible work arrangements'.
>
> Even if we think we don't, as leaders we can all have our unconscious biases. What is your version of 'Girls don't like dinosaurs'?

Mixing business with pleasure

Almost every business or personal experience you have had can be turned into a story. You do not have to manufacture, spin or make up stories. You can simply craft your existing experiences into stories. While we have presented business stories and personal stories as two separate categories, sometimes the distinction is blurry.

For example, you could share a story of how Richard Branson conducts business. But if you came across this in a book you were reading while on holidays, it becomes a business story with a personal context. In instances such as this we would say don't split hairs trying to categorise your story. If it works for your purpose and audience then absolutely use it. In most instances it will be pretty easy to separate personal experiences from business experiences and if there are a few instances where it is not so clear, we can all live with that.

> *I never think of stories as made things; I think of them as found things. As if you pull them out of the ground.*

> **Stephen King, author**

Now, with purpose and audience in mind, scan through and list some of your business and personal experiences to see which of these you could turn into a story using the tools we provide in the next section. A project leader we worked with used the time during a long-haul flight to make a list of several business and personal experiences in one column of an Excel spreadsheet. Then he listed all the purposes for which he needed stories in another column and matched experiences to purposes to craft his stories using the story formula that we will cover next.

The proven story formula

So far you have your story purpose, you have profiled your audience and you have a personal or business experience in mind. Now we will craft your experience into a story using a story-structure formula.

Every story has a classic three-part structure:

- a beginning
- a middle
- an ending.

Let's look at each part in detail.

The beginning

The beginning of a story is a make-or-break situation. In storytelling, in journalism and in speechwriting, your beginning is one of the most important things to consider carefully. In business storytelling it is important that your beginning is really crisp. The beginning sets the scene and should hook your audience in immediately. The most efficient way to begin your stories is with time and place.

'Time and place' has an endless number of variations and we use it naturally in our conversational storytelling. For example, 'Yesterday, when I went to yoga...'; 'When I was a kid, we had a trampoline and I remember once...'; 'Ten years ago I took up karate'.

What? What happened to my big, suspenseful, totally captivating beginning? Time and place almost sounds mundane. However, the very fact that you are talking personal — using a personal experience — is a big hook in business. When was the last time someone said to you in business, 'I grew up on a farm and remember one day...', or 'When I was 10 all I wanted was a new bike for Christmas'?

You can — especially when you are advanced in storytelling — aim for a totally 'out there' beginning, but nine times out of 10 we find time and place, even though it sounds ordinary, works to hook your audience into your story. This is one of the key differences between traditional and business storytelling. In traditional storytelling we may spend ages building up a suspenseful beginning, but in business time is of the essence. You are time poor, as is your audience, so we recommend a sharp, punchy beginning using time and place.

The beginning of a story is not long, but it does give your audience a context and sets the scene for what is to follow. It is all the little things that add up in storytelling — and time and place is one of those very important little things. Time and place signals to your audience that this is a true story.

Now let's look at some beginnings you should avoid.

Let me tell you a true story...

Abandon this opening line. It is just not necessary as you can easily start with, 'That reminds me of a time when I went travelling in Japan...' So avoid starting your stories with 'Let me tell you a (true) story'. It could leave your audience wondering why you said this and they may think the story is possibly not true or that all your other stories are not true.

Once upon a time...

Never start with 'Once upon a time' unless you are talking to a child aged five or younger. Westpac Banking Corporation was slammed in the press when, in 2009, they sent an animated video to all their customers in an attempt to explain why their rates were increasing. It was wrong on many levels, but the initial, most glaring error was that they started with 'Once upon a time...' To their educated, adult customer base struggling with rising interest rates during the global recession it was both patronising and condescending... and completely unnecessary.

The middle

The middle of your story is where all the action happens. When crafting the middle there are a few things you need to consider that will really help your story be effective and efficient.

Where's Wally?

Remember the *Where's Wally?* books? They are the ones where you scan pages full of pictures looking for Wally. In your stories we are going to ask the same question: Where's Wally? That is: *Who is the single main character in your story?* This could be you or it could be someone else (a high school teacher, your dad, and so on).

The key element for creating an effective story is that it must have a single main or key character. Your story should *never* revolve around a group or a team or a company. The group, team or company can provide the context of the story, but you have to zoom in to one character within this context. Think of every narrative we engage with — from books, to television shows, to popular cinema. They are always about characters, and usually with one key character (the hero). As human beings we relate to other people just like us — not to teams or departments. We want to follow the trials and tribulations of a single character, not an anonymous clump of people. So, ideally, your story should revolve around a single character — and it is okay if the key character is you — and you should always give your character a name.

Giving your character a name is really important as it humanises the story. So, if you are telling a story about your brother, use his name. Don't keep saying 'my brother'. For example, you may start the story with 'My brother, Tony...' But after you have introduced the character, refer to him as 'Tony'. Of course, referring to Mum or Dad or Grandma is fine as that is how we always address them.

Sometimes people are reluctant to use the real names of people due to client confidentiality. We see this a lot in the not-for-profit sector. There are a couple of ways of overcoming this concern.

The first way is to simply ask the person — your client or your colleague — whether you may use their name and share their story. You only need to use their first name and we are sure most people would be more than happy for you to do that.

The second way is to replace the name. So, instead of 'Bill' call him 'John'. *Never ever* say, 'Let's just call him John'. On hearing this, your audience will be distracted the entire time you are telling the story. They will either be wondering whether or not the story is true or trying to figure out who the person really is.

'But doesn't this fly in the face of authenticity?' we hear you ask. Only you can decide that. We do not think it does if you are authentic in your purpose and for some reason cannot find the person to get their permission.

Less is more

The business story is minimalist in its approach. Think Coco Chanel who embodied the philosophy 'Less is more'.

Remember that this is storytelling in a business environment. You do not want people thinking, 'Just get to the point'. To help eliminate unnecessary detail always come back to the purpose. If the detail is important to the purpose leave it in; if it is not, take it out.

We had a client once who was narrating a story about customer service and his example was about a time when he bought a computer at Harvey Norman for his wife. The first minute of his story was spent explaining how his wife wanted a new computer, but as she was not very technically literate he was charged with buying the computer. Not only was this detail irrelevant to his purpose, but it alienated all the women in the audience. Instead, he could have started by saying, 'Yesterday I went to Harvey Norman to buy a computer'. That is all he needed to say.

Feel it, see it

Getting the emotion right in your story helps people care about your message. It makes them feel something. We are wired to feel things for people, not for abstractions.

Although we have talked about the importance of emotion, it is worth emphasising just how important it is to get the emotion right for storytelling success. The key is trying to identify the actual emotion your audience will feel or you want them to feel.

A story is not a story unless it has emotional and sensory data.

We had a client who wanted to use a story to communicate the need to outsource one aspect of her organisation's process. It was not a major outsourcing change where jobs were being lost, so that was not an issue. She correctly identified the emotion that people would be feeling as the fear of letting go: that is, the initial fear of letting someone take control of something that you are currently in control of. She relayed these emotions through a story about teaching her younger brother to drive. It absolutely worked. Everyone in the audience had taught someone else — most of them their son or daughter — to drive and could connect with her story and purpose.

Sensory data helps you paint the picture for the audience. Sensory information creates the virtual reality of storytelling. People actually see the story you are sharing in their mind's eye. Here's an example from Kate Sterritt.

Kate's story

When I was in year 7 I joined a new school. I was quite shy and would not answer questions in class. One day our teacher, Mr Bonato, asked a question in class and a lot of students tried to answer it but couldn't. I thought I knew the answer but was too shy to put my hand up. Mr Bonato perhaps sensed this and asked me what I thought. When I stumbled through my reply, it turned out I had the right answer. He then challenged me saying, 'Kate, why didn't you speak up?' and I replied, 'Because what I was thinking was so different from what everyone else was saying'. Then he told me, 'That is what happened to Christopher Columbus. When everyone thought the world was flat, Columbus was the first to declare the world was round, so you have to back yourself'.

Mr Bonato's words still stay with me today and I believe even if you are going against the grain, have the courage to back yourself.

As you were reading this story, could you imagine year 7 students in a class, perhaps similar to your classroom at that age? Could you see Mr Bonato, maybe wearing glasses, and imagine the kids trying to answer the question, and then Kate's shy response? This is how we see stories. We use sensory data — it is as though the narrator is painting a picture in our mind.

In contrast, in a lot of business communication there is no emotion for our hearts to tap into and no sensory image for our minds to latch onto. For example, terms such as 'best of breed', 'pushing the envelope', 'bench strength' and 'step change' offer a turgid jargon-fest but little else. These are harsh words, we know, but you are paying us to be honest, not nice.

Effective business stories, on the other hand, have the right level of sensory detail. A rule of thumb to ensure you have the right level of detail ('less is more') is to constantly go back to the purpose. As we stated previously, if it is important to the purpose, leave the detail in; if it is not relevant to the purpose, leave it out.

The devil is in the detail

Get all the facts right in your story. Your audience will pick up straight away if the detail is incorrect. They will also detect if you are trying to sugarcoat the situation by leaving out all the negative aspects and just focusing on the positives.

In storytelling, getting every detail right matters. Storytelling requires research to get the facts right.

In one of our workshops a client started his story with 'At the first moon landing in 1968 ...' As soon as the person finished the story lots of people chimed in to say that, actually, the first moon landing was in 1969 — that incorrect detail diminished the impact of the story.

A minor incorrect technical error such as this can leave your audience stranded, distracted by it or correcting it in their heads instead of moving along through your story as you tell it.

So making sure all the details are correct is important: in storytelling the devil really is in the detail.

The ending

Ending your story is like landing a plane: one false move and you could crash and burn. There are three steps to follow when ending your story:

- *the bridge*, which brings your audience back to the business context
- *the link*, which links subtly to the business message (the purpose of the story)
- *the pause* at the end of the story.

The bridge

A bridging sentence works to bring your audience back into the room with you, or back into a business context with you.

The bridge is particularly important when you are telling a personal experience. So if your story is about an African safari, or your childhood, your bridging sentence could be as simple as any one of these:

- 'That reminds me of what we are trying to do at work every day...'

- 'What does going on an African safari have to do with us?'

- 'I am sharing this with you because...'

You are creating a bridge to the next step in your ending, the link.

The link

The link should be the final sentence in your story. It should link back to the purpose, but not directly. This is the tricky bit.

There are many ways to link back to the purpose without doing it directly, for example:

- 'Imagine if...'

- 'I invite you to...'

- 'Just think what we could achieve...'

- 'Wouldn't it be amazing if...'

- 'Imagine the difference we could make if...'

You can actually combine two of these to make a very powerful ending. For example, 'Just think what we could do if we delivered this service every day. Imagine the difference we could make.'

Do not use more than two though because your link should only be one sentence — or two very short ones — to be effective. Anything more is overkill.

It is very important to have a positive link as positive endings inspire people. Even if your story is a bit negative in nature — such as a bad customer experience — it is important to end on a positive note.

So, if for example you are sharing a negative customer experience, you could end by saying, 'I am sharing this with you as no customer should ever have that happen to them. We have the opportunity every day to ensure our customers leave our store singing our praises'. 'I am sharing this with you' is the bridge and the sentence where the negative part stops. The linking sentence, 'We have the opportunity every day ... ' then puts in motion the positive message from your story and links back to your purpose.

You will also notice that story endings are very inclusive, using 'we' instead of 'you': 'Imagine if we could do this' is more inclusive than 'Imagine if you could do this'.

You will also note that story endings are not directive. There has to be a real subtlety with your ending. Try to avoid telling people what they should do, feel or think. Resist the urge to tell them and have faith in the story process.

'I invite you to ...' is more inclusive and respectful than 'I ask you to ...' or 'Can you please start to ...?', which are directive. What do we mean by directive endings? Directive endings look like: 'So the moral of the story is ...' or ' So what I want you to get out of this is ...'

Of course you would never ever use lines such as 'The moral of the story is ...' unless your name is Aesop and you are sharing fables.

Gently guide your audience to your purpose because if you are too directive you will simply not get the engagement you are seeking.

The pause

The very last part of your story—and it is important to consider this as part of your story—is the pause at the end. The pause, of course, applies when you are sharing your story, but we ask you to consider it now when you are thinking about your ending.

After the link, you have either asked people to imagine something or invited them to do something. Give them time to process this—to imagine it, to get engaged in it and to be inspired by it.

The pause at the end of the story is when your audience are making their own connection to your story. It is a very powerful part of the process; it is when all your hard work is coming to fruition.

The pause does not have to be long, but at a minimum try for at least three seconds. This may seem uncomfortable, but get used to it. One technique you can use is to breathe through your nose slowly. It is physically impossible to breathe through your nose and talk at the same time, so just take one long, slow breath through your nose. You do not have to do it loudly as if you are hyperventilating either—just slowly and quietly.

Getting your ending right

Let's look at some common mistakes people make with story endings so you can do your best to avoid them.

There must be an ending

Many people share their story and then it just seems to merge into the next thing they are saying. There does not seem to be a distinct ending to the story. There is no bridge, no link and no pause. The result? Your audience think, 'What the heck was that about?'

Know when to stop

Knowing when to stop your story is important, especially if you want a happy ending.

> *Make sure you have finished speaking before your audience has finished listening.*

Dorothy Sarnoff, American Operatic Soprano

Every story has a bell curve of emotion. By stopping right on the top of the bell curve you get maximum impact. If you continue beyond this point you actually get diminishing returns. The audience gets bored, misses the point or wonders when you are going to finish.

To avoid this, know what your last sentence is and make sure you stop after it.

Don't be too directive

Being too directive — for example, telling your audience what you want them to take away from the story — does not work.

In traditional storytelling, stories often end with, 'The moral of the story is …' This is a directive ending and is not suitable for business storytelling.

You have to trust your audience to get your message. This is hard for most leaders to do as we have been taught to spell everything out for our audience instead of trusting and respecting their intelligence. If you are going to be directive at the end of your story because you think your audience will not get it, don't even bother using a story. Just tell them what you want. Stories do a lot of heavy lifting for you and the white space at the end of a story is when your audience mentally relate the story to their own lives, in effect creating their own stories. If you immediately jump into directive mode you have gone back to commanding and controlling as opposed to engaging and enrolling.

Don't be negative

If you have a negative ending to your story, don't expect a positive reaction. To take a line from the movie *Shrek 2*: 'May all your endings be happy!' We all have a yearning for happy endings, so as a storyteller why cheat your audience of this?

> *If you want a happy ending, that depends, of course, on where you stop your story.*
>
> **Orson Welles, actor and director**

What if I have a great story that has a negative ending? You can still use it. You just have to think of a way of turning the negative ending into a positive one. This seems easier said than done, so here is an example of how to do this.

In one of our workshops Kate constructed the following story.

Hurricane Larry

Last year when I visited the Innisfail branch in Queensland and spoke to Diane she told me about the day Hurricane Larry hit. Diane told me that the branch was significantly damaged, flooded and most of the terminals were not working. It was, however, not as badly damaged as other banks in the area.

She and a few other staff members came in, but many others could not as their homes were significantly damaged and home was where they needed to be.

So the call was put out to staff at nearby branches, who travelled for hours to come and help out.

(continued)

Hurricane Larry (cont'd)

Eventually they got one terminal up and running and with the help of their regional branch members were operational again within the day. Being able to provide much-needed cash and services for the community really made a difference.

It's a shame we have to wait for a hurricane before we demonstrate real teamwork.

You can probably feel that the story ending is negative, but Kate did not know how to make it positive. We worked with Kate on her ending and this is how she decided to end her story.

What Diane saw was the power of teamwork, but we don't need to wait for a hurricane to harness that power. Imagine the difference we could make if the spirit of teamwork was part of what we did, every day.

Your aim as an inspiring storyteller is to ensure your story endings leave people in a positive space.

Bringing it all together

Now let's look at an example of how the beginning, middle and ending all work together.

Let's deconstruct a story we have already shared. This is Darren Whitelaw's story, where his purpose was for leaders in his company to send out fewer emails and talk face to face with people more often.

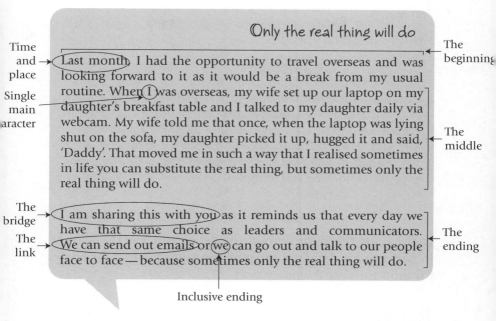

Only the real thing will do

Time and place → Last month, I had the opportunity to travel overseas and was ← The beginning
looking forward to it as it would be a break from my usual
routine. When I was overseas, my wife set up our laptop on my

Single main character → daughter's breakfast table and I talked to my daughter daily via
webcam. My wife told me that once, when the laptop was lying
shut on the sofa, my daughter picked it up, hugged it and said, ← The middle
'Daddy'. That moved me in such a way that I realised sometimes
in life you can substitute the real thing, but sometimes only the
real thing will do.

The bridge → I am sharing this with you as it reminds us that every day we
have that same choice as leaders and communicators. ← The ending
The link → We can send out emails or we can go out and talk to our people
face to face — because sometimes only the real thing will do.

Inclusive ending

First of all, let's find the beginning, the middle and the ending.

The beginning
This is the beginning:

> Last month, I had the opportunity to travel overseas and
> was looking forward to it as it would be a break from my
> usual routine.

It indicates the time and the place quickly and efficiently. It immediately sets the context of the story.

The middle

The middle looks like this:

> When I was overseas, my wife set up our laptop on my daughter's breakfast table and I talked to my daughter daily via webcam. My wife told me that once, when the laptop was lying shut on the sofa, my daughter picked it up, hugged it and said, 'Daddy'. That moved me in such a way that I realised sometimes in life you can substitute the real thing, but sometimes only the real thing will do.

It gives just the right amount of detail and has the specific incident of his daughter hugging the laptop, which brings in the emotional and sensory data.

The ending

This sentence is the bridge:

> I am sharing this with you as it reminds us that every day we have that same choice as leaders and communicators.

This bridging sentence brings us back to reality and explains why Darren is sharing the story.

The link is:

> We can send out emails or we can go out and talk to our people face to face — because sometimes only the real thing will do.

The ending is not directive and is inviting and inclusive. The term 'we' acknowledges that Darren is also not perfect and that he too needs to act on this story's message.

This story really works because it includes all the components of the proven story formula.

What else?

We're not quite there yet...but almost! There are just a few more things to consider when crafting stories.

Write your stories down

Try to get into a habit of writing your stories down. It will bring a real discipline to your storywriting and help you make more educated changes to it. Of course, you will never read your story out when you are presenting it to an audience.

If you are absolutely averse to writing your stories down, you could record your stories on your phone. That way you still have them in a format where you can check that they flow, work together and sound natural.

Name your stories

Once you have written your story down it is important to give it a title so you can recall it easily—for example, 'The copperhead snake' or 'The washing machine story'. However, you should never actually say the title of your story—in other words, do not say, 'I am now going to tell you my copperhead snake story'. Yikes! Naming your stories is more for your personal reference. If we are preparing a client pitch, for example, next to one of the points we may write, 'Share copperhead snake story here'. This is just a quick and easy way to remember it without having to jot the whole story down again.

Don't be surprised when people request their favourite stories again and again using names that they themselves have devised to refer to your stories. They may ask you to narrate 'the snake story' or ask you to share 'the washing machine story'. This just shows how sticky stories are and that people love to hear them again (the good ones, that is).

Story duration and timeline

It is important to ensure your stories do not take too long to tell. We advise that one to two minutes should be the rule of thumb. They can go longer, but you would really have to make sure you have done everything you can to strip out unnecessary detail. Just keep coming back to the purpose. Remember: if it is related to the purpose, keep it in; if it is not, take it out.

You should get into the practice of writing your stories down while you are crafting them as you may need to rework them a couple of times until you get them right.

With regard to the timeline of your story, the beginning should only be one or two sentences. The middle of your story should be the longest part and your bridge and link again only one or two sentences each at the most. Then, of course, you have a pause.

So the breakdown of the duration of your story should look a bit like figure 4.1.

Figure 4.1: story duration breakdown

Beginning	Middle	Ending
5–10%	70–80%	10–20%

TIME

Seek permission

We have touched on this before, but it is important to reiterate that every time you use the names of people in your story, or even share someone else's story, it is important to seek the person's permission first. This does not have to be via both your lawyers, your company's legal counsel or using iron-clad documentation. It can be quite informal: just a face-to face-request or a request via email. The person is most likely to be flattered and agree at once. Sometimes they may want you to use only their first name, which is fine too. Our whole business is built on sharing other people's stories so we know this simple strategy works. Of course, if for whatever reason they do not want you to use their story, please respect their wishes.

Give credit where credit is due

Other times you may be using a story that you read or heard about. It is very important to acknowledge the source. Alternatively, you can use a simple statement such as, 'I remember once hearing about...' or 'I recently read...', or even saying something like, 'I'm not sure where I heard this, but...'

Of course, if you know who used the story first then please credit them. Our mentor Matt Church from Thought Leaders Global calls this 'attribute with honour'. Honour your source, honour your audience by sharing the source with them and stay honourable yourself by doing so. This does not in any way diminish the story or its impact.

Credit your stories and stay credible.

One of our clients shared with us how a presenter launched into a session with a personal story that had them all wowed. The very next day, another presenter shared the exact same story but credited it by saying, 'This is something I read about'. Needless to say, the credibility of the first presenter was destroyed.

Story checklist

It is good practice to test your stories after you have written them. Use this checklist every time you need to test and refine a story.

- ☑ Is your purpose clear and is there only one purpose? (Single message; bumper sticker.)

- ☑ Who is your audience, what motivates them and what are their concerns?

- ☑ Have you picked a personal or business experience to convert into a story?

- ☑ Structure your story so it starts with time and place.

- ☑ Never begin with, 'Let me tell you a true story...' or 'Once upon a time...'

- ☑ Where's Wally? Who is the single key character in your story?

- ☑ 'Less is more': think Coco Chanel and eliminate all unnecessary detail from your story.

- ☑ Feel it, see it. Is there emotional and sensory data in your story?

- ☑ The devil is in the detail so get all your facts right.

- ☑ Does the story link back to the purpose without being directive?

☑ Have you written the story down?

☑ Give your story a title.

☑ Check your story's duration and timeline.

☑ Seek permission if necessary.

☑ Credit your story if needed and stay credible.

This checklist is not a straightjacket; you do have room to move, but we find that when leaders' stories do not quite work, it is usually due to something in this checklist not having been considered. We would strongly recommend using the checklist to test your stories, to ensure they are as inspiring as they can be.

In a nutshell

Did you get hooked?

→ When crafting your story, first ensure you have a very clear purpose on why you are telling your story. You should be able to articulate your purpose with zero corporate jargon.

→ Audience analysis is essential for your story to work. You need to understand what their concerns are and what motivates them.

→ You can find stories in all aspects of your life — from your early childhood to the current day—and it is the everyday experiences that can be the most powerful.

→ All your stories should have a beginning, and a good way to start your stories is with time and place. Avoid using 'Let me tell you a story …' and never start with 'Let me tell you a true story …'

→ The middle of your story is where you have all the detail. It should make the audience feel something (emotion) and see something (sensory data).

→ The ending is crucial to the effectiveness of your story. The ending consists of the bridge statement, the linking back to purpose statement and the pause at the end.

→ Stories should only take about one or two minutes.

→ Writing your stories down and naming them is a good practice to adopt as well as seeking permission if you are using other people's stories or names.

How hooked are you?

→ Think of a message that you want to deliver where a story could help you: a message on a new strategy, the reason for change or simply to get people to update a project plan.

→ Write down the purpose in very simple, non-jargon language and then convert it into a bumper sticker.

→ Assess the audience for your message. Who are they? What motivates them? What are their concerns?

→ Scan through your business or personal life to find an example that could fit your purpose and audience.

→ Take your example through the proven story formula (using the story checklist) to craft your story.

→ Write your story down, taking particular care with the ending.

→ Give your story a name and run it through the checklist again.

Now that we have looked at how to craft your stories, in the next chapter we are going to show you how to make your stories have the greatest impact possible.

CHAPTER 5

Making your stories shine

If you always put limits on everything you do, physical or anything else, it will spread into your work and into your life. There are no limits. There are only plateaus, and you must not stay there, you must go beyond them.

Bruce Lee, martial artist and actor

So you have a good story, but how can you ensure you have an inspiring story — one that is going to land you that multimillion-dollar deal, get you promoted, help you exceed your sales targets or make you the stand-out speaker at your next company event?

If you want to achieve all that and more, this is the chapter for you. We want to make sure your stories 'shine' to give you every chance of getting people hooked on you and your messages.

Avoiding story roadblocks

One of the first things you have to do is to ensure you do not have any 'roadblocks' in your stories. A roadblock is a point in your story where the audience gets stuck.

One presenter we watched shared a story where she was shopping on Thursday and was rushing as the shops shut at 5 pm. Everyone was thinking, 'Thursday is late night shopping. The shops are open until nine'. Immediately there was a roadblock that distracted the audience and made them think, 'You haven't got your details right. Is the rest of your story true?'

Examples of roadblocks include:

- incorrect details
- far-fetched facts
- sensitive subjects
- cultural cringes.

Let's look at each of these in detail.

Incorrect details

A client of ours once started a story with, 'At the 2000 Athens Olympics...' Yeah, right. *Big* mistake. The 2000 Olympics were held in Sydney. Even worse, the majority of his audience lived in Sydney so everyone knew that the date was incorrect. From the moment he said it, this was the only thing anyone could think about.

Mistakes such as this can be really costly. For starters, they undermine your credibility. If he got that fact wrong, his audience may be thinking, 'What else did he get wrong?' Not only that, but imagine if you were pitching to a new client and they had worked on the Sydney Olympics! It would make you look sloppy and incompetent.

Far-fetched facts

One of our clients, Sonia, was sharing a customer-service story about a colleague who was making an urgent delivery to a customer in a remote part of Tasmania. The road was blocked by a fallen tree so her colleague got his chainsaw out of the boot of his car, cut away the tree, cleared the path and continued on to the customer.

Do you carry around a chainsaw in the boot of your car? No, neither do we, nor do the majority of the audience she was talking to. Fortunately, Sonia sensed everyone's disbelief and made a joke about the fact that while it sounded unusual to have a chainsaw in your car, it was quite common if you lived and worked in this remote part of Tasmania. She said, with a roll of her eyes, 'Yeah, I know — a chainsaw in the boot of your car? Only in Tasmania!' The audience laughed and moved through the rest of the story with her.

If there is anything that sounds far-fetched in your story — even if it is true — make sure you have a line explaining it, as Sonia did.

Sensitive subjects

Remember that the point of business storytelling is to evoke an emotional response in your audience. However, there are some subject areas that you have to be extra careful and empathetic with. Serious illness, loss of a loved one and anything that may draw up painful emotions or memories for people can be quite confronting and should be dealt with carefully.

It is common, for example, for someone to talk about their spouse going through cancer and not reveal until the end that their loved one is now okay. Building this type of suspense may work in the movies, but in general this tends to leave your type of audience feeling anxious and unable to concentrate on anything else you are saying.

The way around this is to reveal your ending at the start. For example, you could start your story with, 'Five years ago my daughter was diagnosed with anorexia. I am happy to say she is fit and healthy now, but it was one of the most horrendous times of my life'. Then you can continue to share the story with that roadblock removed.

What if there was no happy ending? This is your moment of truth as a storyteller. You have to decide whether to use the story, whether despite the unhappy ending it will work for your purpose and audience. But do test it with a trusted adviser first to ensure this is the case.

Cultural cringes

Have you ever told a really bad, inappropriate joke and wished you could take it back? Anything surrounding race, religion and gender is, quite frankly, a no-go zone. As a note of caution, what *you* find okay, someone else might find demeaning.

Take for example Tim Mathieson, the partner of Australian Prime Minister Julia Gillard. In January 2013, he was hosting a reception for the touring West Indian cricket team. Being a men's health ambassador, Mathieson was talking about the importance of men having regular check-ups for prostate cancer. He said, 'We can get a blood test for it, but the digital examination is the only true way to get a correct reading on your prostate, so make sure you go and do that, and perhaps look for a small Asian female doctor is probably the best way'. In the room there was laughter, but the media had a field day.

Tony Wright from the Melbourne *Age* newspaper wrote, 'Uh oh. In three words, he'd contravened an expansive sweep of the proposed anti-discrimination decrees. Small (sizeist, you might think); female (sexist); Asian (racist). We won't even go near digital penetration'. Wright added that it was not Mathieson's first offence with badly chosen language.

What can seem like a perfectly innocent attempt at humour can backfire, especially if it has even the slightest hint of sexism or racism — for example, someone telling a story about his wife and referring to her as 'the missus' may sound acceptable to him, but it is a roadblock for some people (especially women) and sends the wrong message about you as the storyteller. In this instance, it says that you are out of touch because you used old-fashioned, sexist language.

Once you have checked your story for roadblocks and removed the roadblocks using the techniques we have suggested, what next? Another way to make your stories shine is to use appropriate humour.

Using humour with purpose

A joke is a very serious thing.

Winston Churchill, former British Prime Minister

Everyone likes a story and everyone likes a funny story but don't slide back to being a Joker (you will remember this term from the Dolan Naidu Story Intelligence Model in chapter 3) by using humour without purpose ... and without a reason. You have come too far to weaken now. Stay strong.

Humour definitely has its place in business storytelling and we encourage you to use it — just use it purposefully.

Let's look at when and why you would use humour in your stories.

Begin with an icebreaker

Humour is scientifically proven to have physical benefits. There is wisdom in the old adage that 'laughter is the best medicine' because laughter:

- relaxes the whole body
- decreases stress hormones

- triggers the release of endorphins, which are the body's natural, feel-good hormones.

This is good news for you and your audience! Not only will laughter help you relax, decrease your anxiety levels and increase the happy hormones, but it will have the same effect on your audience.

We were working with a group of four young leaders who had to present at their company's yearly conference. One of the leaders, Paul, was really nervous, even at the practice session. About halfway through his story he had a humorous line, at which we all laughed. After that he continued on with his story, but in a more natural tone. When everyone laughed and Paul also laughed, it relaxed him and his story flowed better after that.

We suggested to Paul that he should move the humorous line forwards when telling his story, to settle his nerves sooner. This helped him relax into his story significantly earlier, making for a much more engaging story.

Lighten a heavy situation

Sometimes you can lighten an otherwise heavy-going or tense story by weaving in a line to lighten it. This is like having shades of grey, black and white in your story.

In her TED video 'The power of vulnerability', research professor and speaker Brené Brown shares a poignant moment when she had to put data away and find a therapist. She says that she asked five of her friends if they could recommend anyone and they all jokingly implied that no-one would ever want to be her therapist! Brené continues by saying that when she saw the therapist she said to them, 'But here's the thing, no family stuff, no childhood s**t. I just need some strategies'! This is a topic that could have left the audience feeling uncomfortable, but by including humour in her speech Brené was able to make the audience laugh and lighten the atmosphere in the room.

You may be able to pre-empt a heavy situation and have a line in your story ready to go at the appropriate point in your story, as Brené Brown did. It is important to try and lighten the situation to enable your audience to become engaged in your story and not distracted by any dark or uncomfortable elements.

Bring in humility

When you are sharing stories about yourself, it is a good idea to avoid stories about how great you are. Even if the story does involve you doing great things, you can use humour to bring in humility.

This does not mean you have to belittle your achievements, but some self-deprecating humour never goes astray. For example, we heard someone share a story of when they won their club's 'best and fairest' and then added, 'I know you may find that hard to believe looking at me now'.

Next we are going to take this a whole notch up by opening your eyes to how you can pick and select stories for maximum impact.

Negative and positive stories

The stories you tell can be either positive or negative. As a storyteller, it is important to understand the benefits and limitations of both positive and negative stories and in which situations you would use one over the other.

Negative stories

A negative story is usually about a negative event with an unhappy ending. It starts negatively, stays negative and ends negatively. For example, here is a story a leader shared when attempting to explain to his team the importance of doing things the right way.

> ## Doing it the right way
>
> Earlier this year I went overseas with my family. During the weeks leading up to our big overseas adventure I wrote myself a list of all the clothes I would need to take and advised my wife and two teenage kids to do the same. They kept assuring me they had everything under control, but on the first night, on landing in a freezing New York city, it became obvious that neither my wife nor my daughters had packed appropriate warm-weather gear. The next day I had to spend a fortune on buying them all coats, gloves and scarves. If they had followed the procedure I recommended and been better prepared, this would not have happened. We are planning another trip next year and this time I am going to take control of the packing.

The story is negative because it starts off negatively and does not get any better. The ending implies a level of blame towards the leader's wife and daughters. Hearing it does not leave the listener in a good place.

We have an abundance of negative stories around us ... they have a life of their own. There is a saying around customer-service issues that if someone is happy with your products they will tell one person; if they are unhappy they will tell 10 people. You do not need a communications plan to circulate negative stories ... they spread like wildfire. This is why it is so important to understand their purpose and their limitations.

Negative stories have a very specific purpose. They can shock people into seeing a situation differently, they can create a sense of urgency and they can carry lessons. They raise awareness of a situation, especially if no-one currently thinks there is even a problem.

To use negative stories well is to understand that they only inform people — they do not influence behaviour. At best, you may get begrudging compliance by telling negative stories, but if you want long-term change of behaviour they are not going to be as effective as positive stories because negative stories inform, but they do not influence. If you want to influence behaviour in a positive direction and for the long term, you have to use positive stories.

Negative stories have limitations so to inspire action and change behaviour, you need to follow your negative story with positive stories. You may need a negative story first to shock your audience and raise awareness of a problem. But if you leave it at that, you may do no more than raise awareness of a problem (which is fine if that is all you want to achieve).

Sharing his own experiences, Harvard Business School professor John Kotter states, 'I concluded years ago that people need more positive examples than negative ones. People are seeing too much negative stuff, and they know it. They can all give you 53 negative stories. What people need are positive examples of what works'.

So it is important to understand that the purpose of negative stories is to grab people's attention; they inform people, raise awareness of a situation or create a sense of urgency. It is also important to understand their limitations. They will not change behaviour. To achieve that you need to follow your negative story quickly with positive stories.

Positive stories

A positive story can present a challenge or deal with adversity; the positive part comes from how the problem was overcome and presents a positive or happy ending.

This does sound trite, but when done well it is simple, effective and powerful. We are all hooked on popular television shows, movies and books that embrace what American scholar Joseph Campbell first described as 'The Hero's Journey'. This is a narrative pattern that describes the typical adventure of the archetype known as The Hero, who faces challenges and overcomes them.

Some positive stories are positive all the way through; others have the 'hero's journey' structure. So while a negative story starts negatively, stays negative and ends negatively, a positive story can start either positively or negatively. If it does start negatively it then turns positive and it always ends positively.

Unlike negative stories, there is sadly a dearth of positive stories. *Huffington Post* is trying to remedy this by running a section described as 'A spotlight on what's inspiring, what's positive and what's working, *Huffington Post* Good News covers the stories that most media chooses not to'. Have a look at www.huffingtonpost.com/good-news for inspiration on positive stories.

Negative or positive?

Of course not all stories will fit neatly into one of these two categories. Sometimes the distinction will be fuzzy. What helps decide is how the story ends. Does it leave the listener in a better place than when the story started? If so, it is more likely to be a positive story. If you are not sure about a story, but you feel it is right for your audience and purpose we would still recommend using it and not forcing it into one category or the other. For the stories that do fit into one of these categories — negative or positive — what we share with you next will help gauge their impact.

The Story Impact Matrix

So, your stories can be either positive or negative and — as we shared in chapter 4 — they can be either business or personal. Your business story could, for example, be either of a customer not using your product and suffering the consequences (negative) … or of a customer using your product and gaining the benefits (positive). It is the same with your personal stories … they can be either positive or negative.

When we add positive and negative to the mix we end up with four different types of stories:

- the negative business story
- the positive business story
- the negative personal story
- the positive personal story.

We have combined these into The Story Impact Matrix (as shown in figure 5.1, overleaf). This matrix will help you choose the right story for maximum impact easily and it can also be used after the event to assess the impact of your story, as well as other people's stories.

Figure 5.1: The Story Impact Matrix

The positive business story medium effectiveness	**The positive personal story** very high effectiveness
The negative business story low effectiveness	**The negative personal story** medium effectiveness

The negative business story

Negative business stories serve a purpose as they teach a lesson or raise awareness of a problem. Their limitation is that they have a low rate of effectiveness. Follow your negative business story with either a positive business story or a positive personal story.

This is an example of a negative business story that a leader who worked in a call centre told her team.

> ### Lack of ownership
>
> Last week I rang my mobile phone company and I was on the phone for what felt like forever. It was such a long wait time and it made me feel really frustrated. It is not like when you go into a shop and you can see people serving customers... in that situation you can see how many people are in the queue in front of you. Being on the phone makes the wait seem even longer and I just started to feel like no-one was concerned about me... that I didn't matter. When I eventually got through, the operator I spoke to was lovely, but it took me three phone calls to get my problem resolved. I reflected on this and thought, this is exactly what our customers must feel: long wait times and lack of ownership.

This story is negative because there is nothing really positive in the whole story and it does not leave the listener with any sense of hope that things can change. This story is also likely to start a downward spiral of people sharing their own negative experiences with phone companies.

The positive business story

The positive business story is more effective than the negative business story simply because it leaves you in a better, more positive, happier place. Here is an example (overleaf).

The new iPhone

After getting my new iPhone, I was having trouble syncing my emails. I tried to find a solution by looking online but in the end thought I had better just ring Apple. I hate ringing help centres because, first, you are normally left hanging on the line forever and, second, they usually cannot fix your problem. I called Apple and was pleasantly surprised how quickly my call was answered. I spoke to a very polite man and after about 10 minutes he advised me that what I was trying to do could not be done. I hung up feeling a bit disappointed that my problem was not resolved, but I probably did not expect anything more. A few minutes later my phone rang and it was another person from the Apple help desk. She advised me that the advice I had just been given was incorrect and I could in fact do what I wanted. Within minutes my emails were syncing and she apologised for the initial incorrect advice. I can't describe how overwhelmed I was that a call centre had called back, fixed my problem and exceeded all my expectations. Imagine if our customers felt this every single time they dealt with us!

The story is positive because even though everything did not go perfectly, obstacles were overcome and the end leaves the listener in a place where things are possible.

The negative personal story

A negative personal story is where you tell a negative story with a personal example.

The story about packing for a trip to New York we shared previously is an example of a negative personal story. It starts negatively, stays negative and offers no hope at the end.

The positive personal story

The positive personal story is the most effective type of story. This is because it combines the influential power of positivity with the connectedness and higher recall of a personal example.

Here is an example from one of our clients, Fiona Michel, who worked for a company that had a global parent company with a different brand. Her team often felt torn between the local company and the global company. This is a positive personal story she shared to get the message across that feeling torn was okay.

The fish pie

A couple of years ago I was away with two friends for a winter weekend getaway. It was freezing cold and the conversation turned to what was the best comfort food. We all agreed it was fish pie, but my two friends then had a debate about the best fish pie recipe. The debate turned into a cook-off, with me being in the fabulous position of not having to lift a finger in the kitchen but being asked to judge which was the best fish pie.

My two friends toiled away in the kitchen with much humour, passion and secrecy. The first fish pie I tasted was very much the traditional kind of fish pie I was used to. It used smoked fish with peas in a thick, rich sauce. It was absolutely fantastic. The second pie was less traditional and more gourmet, with fresh fish in a light, creamy sauce and parsley. It was different from the first but equally delicious. I could not make a choice; both fish pies were great — different, but great — so I didn't make a choice. We all just sat back and enjoyed both of them.

(continued)

> ## The fish pie (cont'd)
>
> I often think back to this wonderful night when I hear our people feeling pulled between our two brands. We feel confused because we think we have to choose, but we don't have to make a choice between the two brands. Just think of the benefits we can enjoy by not choosing and accepting the delights that both can bring.

This is a perfect example of a positive personal story and it highlights that inspiring business storytelling is not about business stories but rather how you can take personal stories and relate them to a business message. After many years of research we can confidently advise you that these are always the most effective stories... always.

So there you have the four kinds of stories. We are not suggesting that you have to use a positive personal story all the time because the type of story you tell will depend on your purpose and message. But if you are finding that your positive business or negative personal stories are not quite hitting the mark, give a positive personal story a go.

It is also good to have a mix. You may even have two stories for the same purpose, which means you can test them out and see which one delivers you greater success.

In order to make your stories resonate you have to consider your purpose and audience. As a storyteller you have to choose the best type of story for your purpose and audience from the types in The Story Impact Matrix (see figure 5.1 on p. 98).

So remember that you have the following choices:

- *The negative business story* raises awareness to a problem, but may not change behaviour.

- *The positive business story* is still in the business realm so you can stay in the logic space and create audience pushback.

- *The negative personal story* is refreshing as it is personal — not business related — and may engage, but it may not inspire because it is negative.

- *The positive personal story* is refreshing because it is personal; people can relate to it and it inspires and engages because it is positive.

The magic of storytelling lies in making your story as realistic as possible. When we talk about realism on various levels, we come across the concept of story matching.

Story matching

Matching is a subtle aspect of storytelling. Matching can refer to:

- language
- age of character
- era and character.

Let us explain each of these for you.

Language

When you are telling a story, the language your key character speaks should match who they are. If you were narrating a story on customer service, it would sound wrong for the customer-service assistant to say, 'We do that for every customer because that is our retail strategy'. That sounds like a bit of scripting, even if the person actually did say that. The language you use must appear consistent with something they would actually say in real life. For example, the customer-service assistant may say, 'We do that for every customer because it makes each of them feel special'. This simple language matching makes your story credible and authentic.

Age of character

When Australian Prime Minister Julia Gillard made a speech to the US Congress in 2011 she talked about how for her own generation, the defining image of the United States was the first landing on the moon. She remembered how she and her classmates were sent home from school to watch the great moment on television. She would have been about five years old when this happened and she used language appropriate for that age when she said, 'I'll always remember thinking that day, Americans can do anything'.

Quite often people's stories are about when they were children. So if you are narrating a story about when you were 10 years old, you have to use language that a 10 year old would use, as this reflects the age of the character.

Era and character

If your character is from, say, the 1960s or 1970s you have to match the language or pop-culture references to that era (without being corny, of course). For example, phrases such as 'Far out, dude!', 'Groovy, baby!', 'Peace' and 'Flower power' would be appropriate. Think disco, mood rings, lava lamps and tie dye. You could not, for example, have someone from the 1960s saying 'As if', 'Whatever' or 'OMG'.

When you are narrating a story set in a particular era, your character must also fit into the era. If you were talking about when you went to your first interview in the 1980s, this could be as simple as the character saying, 'I remember both the interviewer and I had shoulder pads and big hair'. This makes the whole story come together and sets the right scene for your story and your character.

Match your story to a purpose

One of our clients once narrated a story of going through a major illness and then linked that to what a lot of people would consider a mundane business matter (the purpose). There was a lack of connection between the level of the story and the business purpose of the story. Everyone in the room was most likely thinking, 'When you've been through something like that, a small business matter like this one shouldn't matter'.

On a separate occasion, we heard a leader narrate a story on losing someone close to them. They followed with the message that this had always given them a perspective on what is important in life—their family and people. This story worked because the speaker took something significant and linked it to a significant message, not to something trivial.

Most people match the level of their story to its purpose intuitively. But it is always worth checking this, especially if your story is about a serious life crisis such as a major illness.

In a nutshell

Did you get hooked?

→ Roadblocks in your stories can stop people moving with you through your story. Potential roadblocks include incorrect detail, far-fetched facts, sensitive subjects and cultural cringes.

→ Humour has a place in your storytelling if used purposefully. Humour can be used to break the ice. It can be used to lighten a heavy situation and to bring in humility for you as the storyteller. Jokers in particular need to ensure they are not being self-indulgent with humour and using it without purpose.

→ Stories can be either negative, positive or a bit of both.

→ As well as negative or positive, stories can also be personal or business. Positive personal stories are the most inspiring.

→ Matching is very important when you are storytelling. You need to match the language you use to ensure it is relevant to your key character and the era of the story. You also need to match the level of your story to its purpose.

How hooked are you?

→ Take the story you crafted in chapter 4 and make sure there are no potential roadblocks in it.

→ If you already use some stories as a leader, review them against The Story Impact Matrix and if they are not giving you the results you want, think about how you could use a positive personal story instead.

In this chapter we left no stone unturned to ensure your stories will have the greatest impact possible. In the next chapter we are going to look at what you can do to deliver them like a natural-born storyteller.

CHAPTER 6

Practising and delivering stories

*My best ad libbed stories have been practised for
hours in front of the mirror.*

**John Stewart, Chairman, Legal and General, London
and Director, Telstra Corporation, Melbourne**

Once you have done all the hard work of crafting your
stories you should get into the practice of practising them.
Yes, we can hear you groaning, but practice is the secret
sauce of storytelling: practise, practise and then some
more practise. Never for a moment be seduced by anyone
who seems a natural at storytelling; it is practice that got
them there.

Practice ensures you deliver your stories with impact and,
sadly, there is no shortcut. And no app has been invented as
yet that can do it for you or that can take the place of good,
old-fashioned practice.

In this chapter we are going to look at the best way to practise
and deliver your stories. This could be delivering your
stories in a presentation, seguing naturally into a story in a
meeting, in a corridor conversation or during a one-on-one
coaching session — in fact, it could occur in practically any
business context.

Practising your story

You cannot just 'wing it' when you tell stories in business. You have to practise your stories and then pull them out at just the right moment. Just as a rabbit has to be in the hat in order for a magician to pull it out, you have to craft and practise your stories so that you are prepared to tell them whenever the opportunity arises.

We know you are time poor and keen for quick results so next we are going to share some fast and easy practice techniques. As Canadian hockey player Eric Lindros said, 'It's not necessarily the amount of time you spend at practice that counts; it's what you put into the practice'. We suggest committing to these practice techniques to experience some dazzling results.

Practise, practise, practise!

Practice always starts with writing your story down. We covered this earlier, but we cannot stress how important it is. Once you have a written-down version of your story, there are two levels of practice to embrace.

The first level is where you practise solo. This is where you narrate your story, say it out loud and listen to it. This could be in the shower, while walking the dog or while driving the car. It is very important to speak your story out loud as you would in a real-life situation. Just practising in your head is not the same thing and it will not give you the same results.

We know this may make you cringe, but a private setting such as your car or the shower provides an embarrassment-free, safe space for practising aloud. You can also speak your story out loud, record it into your phone and listen back to it. Practising in front of the mirror does work for some people, but it can make others self-conscious. Pick the technique that works best for you.

No matter how well prepared you are, the words will not come out right the first time. Not even the second time. So you have to practise.

Practising solo and hearing yourself tell your story ensures the story works for you. You will know if it feels right and flows naturally and you will change it accordingly. Sometimes a word may not sit just right with you when you verbalise it; this is an opportunity to tweak your story.

Once you have practised a few times on your own, the next level of practice is to practise in front of someone else. This could be your partner, your kids or preferably a trusted colleague at work. Practising with even just one other person takes your story from being something static to being something dynamic. When we engage another person in our story we automatically alter it by changing our pace and tuning into their non-verbal body language.

The person you practise in front of can also give you honest and constructive feedback. Practising for real allows you to get a better indication of how long the story actually takes and it helps you determine your pace. It makes it all come alive. It also gives you more confidence when you actually use your story with your real audience.

> *Practice isn't the thing you do when you're good.*
> *It's the thing you do that makes you good.*

Malcolm Gladwell, *Outliers: The Story of Success*

Remember: practice makes perfect. The more you practise, the more effective your story will be. So never worry that by practising your story you will make it sound too perfect. It is your story and you will vary it slightly with each telling so it will never sound like something learned by rote.

So there you have it. To be a natural storyteller — or at least look and sound like a natural one — you have to prepare and practise. We know preparation and practice does not sound very sexy. But storytelling, like any other skill, can be taught and learnt ... and we can all improve.

Storytelling practice checklist

Here are our top tips for practising storytelling:

- ☑ Write your stories down.
- ☑ Practise aloud and alone in your car, in the shower or in front of the mirror.
- ☑ Practise in front of someone.
- ☑ Practise some more!

As golf player Gary Player once famously said, 'The more I practise, the luckier I get'.

If you are still not convinced about the power of practising your stories, then let us introduce you to Jody Clark, who was asked to present to her local Rotary club.

Jody had to present for 20 minutes and was completely overwhelmed at the prospect. She wanted to share a story that was significant in her life and that demonstrated the values she had.

Jody had never spoken about herself in such a public forum before and was pretty nervous, so what she did was practise, practise and practise some more. She practised out loud to herself, she practised in front of her family and she recorded herself on her iPad.

After the presentation Jody told us, 'It was so amazing; it was like magic! As soon as I started to share the story about my dad not coming home from the 1990 grand final for three days I could just see everyone looking at me and I could feel they were really engaged in my story. In the end, I can't believe how easy it was and I would really love to do it again. I know it was all the preparation and practice that made it easy and it was all worth it because I was on such a high all day'. This is the story she told.

Jody's story

I want to take you back to the 1990 AFL Grand Final where Collingwood versed Essendon. My father, a mad keen Collingwood supporter, was so excited that day, dressed in his suit and ready to head off to the grand final. I remember Mum fixing his tie and saying, 'Have a great day'...and off he went.

Collingwood won and Dad never came home that night. He just didn't come home. The next morning he still had not arrived. Mum said he was probably still out celebrating. All of Sunday went by and still no Dad. Monday morning we woke up...and still no Dad.

By this stage we were starting to get worried and were going to file a missing person's report. That Monday night we put on the news and they crossed live to Collingwood's home ground where there was still a sea of supporters celebrating 48 hours after the win. And there we saw my dad in the background singing 'Good Old Collingwood Forever'!

So we knew he was still alive, but he was still not home. At 6 am on Tuesday he came home and collapsed on the couch. He said to Mum, 'I'm not feeling too well. I think you'd better take me to hospital'. As you can imagine, a heated discussion followed and at Dad's insistence, Mum finally took him to hospital where the doctors advised us he had suffered a minor stroke.

(continued)

Jody's story (cont'd)

Dad is still alive and well and still a mad Collingwood supporter, but I am sharing this with you because this event provides a great insight into my childhood and how I was raised. There was no doubt that I was loved and cared for, but often we were left to fend for ourselves. This independence saw me volunteering at a hospital when I was 15 years of age and is why today — 30 years later — I am running my own business.

Jody told us that telling this story was one of the highlights of her life.

Delivering your story

Story delivery is where the rubber hits the road. This is the moment of truth and your opportunity to inspire and make a difference. But before we delve into the secrets of the perfect delivery, a word about a very normal feeling: anxiety.

Dealing with anxiety

You may feel a level of anxiety when you are just about to narrate your story... and this can happen at a team meeting or a big town hall meeting, a sales meeting, when you are pitching for a multimillion-dollar tender, or even during a one-on-one corridor chat.

We want you to know that feeling anxious is completely normal. Trust us on this: we have felt anxious and nearly every one of our clients has told us they have felt anxious too. Anxiety usually happens because you have put so much effort into your story. You have prepared and practised it and, most importantly, you really want it to work. But there is a part of you that is thinking, 'What if they don't get it?' With all of that going on, it is no surprise that some anxiety creeps in.

We believe a level of anxiety is a good thing because it is an indicator that you really want your story to work. As long as the anxiety does not develop into crippling fear, you will be fine.

We have only had one client come and tell us that she was so anxious that she could not tell her story. Ironically, her story was about 'taking the bull by the horns' and just giving something a go. She bitterly regretted missing that opportunity, and vowed never to let that happen again.

Delivery techniques

So, you have practised and dealt with you anxiety issues. Now it is time to deliver your story. Next we will give you some tips to help you deliver your story in the most effective way possible.

Never read out your stories

Never ever read out your stories. You may remember that we recommended you write your stories down as a way of recording them. This is not for the purpose of reading them out when you are presenting. Reading your stories out causes your audience to disconnect from them. Because the story is yours, you will find it easy to remember and if you have practised it, your delivery should just flow. So never ever read your story out. Then if you do get something slightly wrong, the only person who will know about it is you.

Believe in your stories

You have to believe in the power of your stories before anyone else will. Have faith in the process and know it will work.

Use your normal voice

When you are narrating your stories, try to avoid adopting a 'story voice'. You would be surprised to know how many intelligent, sophisticated people do that — you know, the 'sing song, once upon a time' voice. Perhaps it is a hangover from reading bedtime stories to our kids. Speak as if you are having a conversation. Just use your normal, everyday talking voice.

Speak to only one person

When you are telling your stories, always narrate them as if you are speaking to just one person. Even if you are talking to 10 or 1000 people, talk as if you are talking to only one. Talking as if you are speaking to just one person will help you connect to every individual in your audience. It is a simple, yet powerful, technique.

Pace yourself

When people are new to storytelling they tend to rush their stories. This is because they still do not fully understand the power of stories and want to race to the end. If you have been disciplined during the preparation of your stories, they will vary in length from one to two minutes, so there is no need to rush. Pace yourself, and your story will be more effective. This will make the whole experience more memorable and enjoyable for everyone.

Pacing your stories correctly takes practice. Some of your stories may start at a slow pace and gradually speed up. Others may be fast from the beginning. You have to play with them and see what works for your purpose, your audience and you.

Take a pause

Most people in business are uncomfortable with silence so they rush in to fill silences. However, both during and after your story pausing can be a powerful tool. We have already talked about including a pause as part of the end of your story. Pauses can also be used effectively during your story, where appropriate. Your pauses should vary in length from two to three seconds to even longer. It may feel like an eternity, but it is not and it helps to build suspense or make a point.

Repeat for effect

Repeating one line from your story can be a very effective way of getting a message across to your audience. Whenever we tell the story of how John Stewart says, 'My best ad libbed stories have been practised for hours in front of the mirror' when he is asked if storytelling comes naturally to him, we repeat the quote a second time. It enhances the message and allows it to sink in. Repetition is, however, a tool to be used sparingly.

Make eye contact

Make eye contact as you are telling your story — not in a 'stare them down' or 'who blinks first loses' way, but in a 'connecting with you', human way.

If you are sharing your story with a larger audience, try to make eye contact with various parts of the room. If there are 100 people in the room you obviously cannot make eye contact with every person, so try to make eye contact with people in different parts of the room.

It is also a good idea not to focus only on the one person who is warmly smiling and already really connected with you. You already have them won over, so focus on others.

Enjoy telling your stories

We once saw a CEO squirm his way through a story. Later, it turned out that he had been cajoled into sharing it by his media adviser. It was painful to watch and about as enjoyable for everyone as root canal treatment. The biggest tip we can give you is to share the stories that you enjoy telling. Your warmth, passion and energy will come through and if you enjoy telling them, you are more likely to keep sharing them.

In a nutshell

Did you get hooked?

→ Being anxious before telling a story is normal. Understand that, know it will happen and simply push through it.

→ Never read out your stories. It creates an immediate lack of connection. You should not have to refer to notes as you know your own stories and you have practised them.

→ Believe in your stories. You have done all the hard work so trust the process and the power of stories.

→ When sharing your stories, use your own voice, and speak as if you are speaking to one person.

→ Pace yourself. Do not rush through your story and remember to pause at appropriate times and repeat lines for impact.

→ Make eye contact when telling your story.

→ Enjoy telling your stories — it will show!

How hooked are you?

Which of these points could you start working on straight away for your next story?

→ Never read out your stories.

→ Believe in your stories.

→ Use your own voice.

→ Speak as if you are talking to one person.

→ Pace yourself.

→ Pause a couple of times.

→ Repeat a line if appropriate.

→ Make eye contact.

→ Enjoy telling your story.

In this chapter we have looked at the importance of practising your stories; provided some easy and fast practice tips; and looked at delivery techniques to help you deliver your stories in a way that will have a real impact, increase your leadership presence and dramatically increase your ability to influence people into action.

In the next chapter we are going to reveal more secrets that will allow you to take your storytelling abilities to the next level.

CHAPTER 7

Secret storytelling business

In order to succeed, your desire for success should be greater than your fear of failure.

Bill Cosby, comedian and actor

Jamie Oliver's cookbook, *Jamie's 15 Minute Meals* not only contains lots of recipes, as you would expect, but it also includes some really useful techniques and tips. One great technique is to construct your salad on the serving platter in layers and then drizzle dressing over the top. Do not mix the dressing through the salad in one bowl and then put it into another salad bowl. This is time-consuming and the salad looks so much better on a platter than in a salad bowl.

Storytelling is similar: there are secrets that no-one talks about which can take your mastery to a whole new level. That's what this chapter will unravel.

Assessing your success

By now you should have prepared at least one story, practised it and, most likely, delivered it. Congratulations!

As soon as you have told a story, the first thing you want to know is, 'Did it work?' We crave that immediate feedback. Sometimes, someone will tell you right away. Or you may find out later … if you are lucky.

Our business mindset demands that we have to be able to measure and identify how effective our story has been. So how do you do this? Do you gather feedback from the audience? Do you evaluate whether there were long, uncomfortable pauses? Was the audience queuing up to ask questions at the end?

We have seen our clients enjoy spectacular results — for example, Michael with his brussels sprouts story (see p. 3). Nevertheless, it is difficult to judge and evaluate how effective your story is immediately after you narrate it. But there are some ways of judging effectiveness.

Sometimes life is perfect and people immediately say, 'Wow!' at the end of your story. In fact, in one of our workshops, when a leader finished narrating a story another leader said, 'Wow!' and took a $50 note out of his wallet, adding 'Here's $50. Can I please use that story?' But you cannot expect instant gratification when you tell your story. This sort of instant feedback is more the anomaly than the rule.

There are times when you may share something with someone and think nothing of it. Then later — perhaps even years or decades later — you see that person and they say something like, 'I still remember that story you told about your dad. It had such an impact on my life'. Don't you love it when that happens?

Good stories have a long tail. We have some clients who thought their stories did not work and six months later someone told them very casually, 'I still remember the story you told us about that horror plane flight you were on'. Or you may get a repeat request out of the blue when someone says, 'John, I really think you should share that story on innovation you told us in last year's forum' ... and poor John had been wondering all that time if his story had resonated with anyone!

Here are some indicators you can look out for both during and after you have told the story.

Audience engagement

Look around the room when you are narrating your story. You should be able to sense the level of engagement in the room.

One of our clients, Alex, described her experience when she started telling a story during a presentation. 'I could not believe it: I started telling the story and every single person was looking at me and I could tell they were really interested. I thought I would be nervous, but it felt so good'.

Another option is to ask someone you trust to observe the audience participation. Prepare them for it by letting them know you are going to share a few stories and ask them to look around the room and gauge the audience's response to see if the stories worked. This person could also collect some feedback for you afterwards by mingling with the audience while they talk about your presentation.

Silence is golden

You finish your story. You pause. Then check: was there also a pause in the room? The silence after your story is golden and normally a good indication of whether it worked or not. Make sure, however, that it is a genuine silence where people are making a connection with your story, and not 'everyone is asleep or has left the building' silence.

Look who's talking

After you have told the story, do you hear of other people repeating it? This may happen and it may not happen immediately, but if it does, it certainly is a good indication that your story has worked.

As you may recall, with a story you are hoping to get people to understand, remember and hopefully retell it without losing its meaning. So hearing others repeat your story, or being told someone has repeated your story, means it has worked. Of course, people may be repeating your stories without you ever knowing about it.

Twitter feeds tell all

If you are sharing stories in a public domain and social media use is encouraged, check the Twitter feed to see what people are saying about the story. Liza Boston, one of our clients, shared a story at a TEDxMelbourne event. After she had told the story, one Twitter comment said, 'Liza Boston's story alone has made the ticket price to this event worth it'.

Reflection for perfection

No matter how good you are at storytelling, you can always get better! How do you keep excelling and going to the next level with your storytelling? There are many ways you can do this, but the most basic premise is reflection.

Champions keep playing until they get it right.

Billie Jean King, champion tennis player

Once you have told your story, reflect on how it went. Did it work? How did you feel? What could you do better?

Your reflection can be done alone, or you can seek feedback from people who heard your story as part of your reflection process. It really does not matter how you do it, what approach you use or how fastidious you are. The key is to reflect, and ideally to do it straight away.

The smaller the window of time that passes between narrating your story and reflecting on it, the more accurate your reflection will be. We are all human and details can get blurred or muddled even within 24 hours. The more time you allow to pass, the less likely you are to come back and reflect on the story. Other more pressing things will take up your time and energy. So the key to reflection success and storytelling excellence is to reflect straight away or as close as possible to when you tell the story.

There are two approaches to reflection that work well for us in storytelling and in life generally. You may have your own approach to reflection, and that is fine. If it works for you, keep doing it. Now think about how you can apply your reflection practice to your storytelling.

The two approaches to reflection that we find useful are:

- The Traffic Signal Approach
- The Story Impact Matrix.

Let's have a look at these two approaches.

The Traffic Signal Approach

The Traffic Signal Approach is a quick way to reflect. It uses the metaphor of road traffic lights.

The red light indicates what you should stop doing when storytelling. This could be as simple as not saying 'um' between words.

The amber light indicates what you should consider changing. This could be, for example, the ending of your story or a particular line in it.

The green light indicates what you should continue doing. This may be retaining the killer beginning.

You will find that if you reflect and incorporate the changes based on The Traffic Signal Approach the next time you tell your story, it will be better than the previous time you shared your story. It is a process of continual improvement. Of course, the more often you tell your story and realise that it works, the less often you will have to reflect on it. But we do recommend it for every new story you tell.

The Story Impact Matrix

Another, more sophisticated, tool you can use to help with your reflection is The Story Impact Matrix, which we described in chapter 5 (see p. 98). Applying the matrix when reflecting on a story could convince you to completely change your story—but that's okay, especially if using the matrix helps you change your story for the better. For example, if you told a positive business story, could you use a positive personal story next time?

Reflection and evaluation are all about improvement, and what better way to improve stories than by using The Story Impact Matrix to increase the impact of every story you tell?

The six Rs of storytelling

Once you have an idea of how your story is working you are in a better position to decide whether you need to change anything about it. Do you retain it and improve it? Or do you retire it?

You can really maximise your return on the investment of time and energy spent creating a story by understanding the six Rs of storytelling, which are:

- reuse stories
- retire stories

- recycle stories
- reject stories
- replenish stories
- retain stories.

Reuse stories

Stories can be reused, but you have to do this in a clever way that works for you, not against you. Reusing stories does not work if you have a handful of stories that you repeat to the same people all the time. We all know someone who does this ('Here comes Stuart with his football story again'). This can make you a story bore. So how can you reuse your stories to help you soar instead of bore?

> *If you've heard this story before, don't stop me,*
> *because I'd like to hear it again.*
>
> **Groucho Marx, comedian**

One way is to reuse your stories with different audiences. You can still use the one story (because you know it works) with different audiences. One word of advice though: you may have to tweak the language slightly to suit your audience.

Michael Brandt (the brussels sprouts hater from chapter 1) used the brussels sprouts story in his region for six months and then stopped using it because everyone had heard it. When he was transferred to another region, he said, 'Guess what? I'm dusting off brussels sprouts again,' and he started telling the same story because this was a completely different audience.

Retire stories

Most good things must come to an end. In this vein you must know when your stories have reached their expiry date. In fact, we strongly recommend retiring your stories just before they hit their expiry date. All stories have a shelf life and you have to be business savvy and know this so that you stop before people start groaning, 'Oh no, not the football story again'. So how do you know when to retire your stories? One marker is when your target audience has heard your story and the message has got through.

Using the example of Michael, he stopped using the brussels sprouts story because his audiences had all heard it and it had entered their daily language. They started achieving and exceeding their sales targets. The purpose of the story had been accomplished.

Remember, you can only aim for your story to reach about 80 per cent of your audience. Don't expect 100 per cent of your audience to 'get it' 100 per cent of the time. That would be unrealistic and no-one deserves that level of influence. Quite often people resist retiring their stories because they are waiting for that 100-per-cent mark. When you try to do that, you end up losing the 80 per cent you had. Don't worry though, retirement need not be a permanent thing. Your stories will not end up in the 'great story graveyard', never to be seen again. Just like John Farnham, your stories can have comebacks too. You can bring your stories out of retirement at any appropriate times. Imagine if you had to do this due to popular demand?

Recycle stories

When you bring stories out of retirement you can recycle them with a different message. Michael could, for example, recycle his brussels sprouts story to get people to keep up with their compliance paperwork. Stories are very environmentally friendly in that regard. And as always the keys are *purpose* and *audience*. As long as you use these to guide you, your recycling efforts should be a resounding success.

Reject stories

Rejecting stories is powerful, but it can be painful or difficult to do. There will be times when you have a fabulous story that you are dying to use. It is exactly at these times that you may have to exercise the greatest self-discipline and reject the story.

So how do you know when to reject a story? You probably know what we believe is the answer to this question because we have mentioned it several times already. Reject the story if:

- *it serves no business purpose.* Telling a story to amuse someone or to fill time is valid in your personal life, but not in business storytelling.

- *it has no clear purpose.* It simply will not work. You have to know the purpose in order to get the message across.

- *it is not appropriate for the audience or the context.*

Rejection does not mean you will never tell the story. Our rejected stories are stored in a file and quite often we think of a purpose that one of the stories could have or an audience for whom the story would be perfect some time down the track.

Replenish stories

You have to keep adding new stories to your story repertoire. We often think of this using the analogy of a library.

Imagine if a library only ever stocked 10 books and never replenished their stock. Similarly, we find when leaders first experience the power of storytelling, they embrace it enthusiastically and craft five stories which they share for five years! 'Stop!' we say. You should replenish your story library every six months. Add new stories in so your stock is always fresh and inspiring.

Retain stories

Finally — and most importantly — know which of your stories are 'gold' and always retain them in your business across everything you do. These are the stories that give you results every time. For us it is the brussels sprouts story from chapter 1 (as you may have already guessed!). Once you have these golden stories, start looking for applications for them. Use them in sales, to pitch to customers, on your website and in corridor chats. Never lose sight of these golden stories. They are the golden goose that will lay you golden eggs in terms of business rewards and success. You have worked really hard to find, write and practise these stories, and they will pay you back richly.

Aligning stories with actions

The one thing you need to be absolutely sure of when you start actively using stories is that your stories are congruent with your actions. This is essential.

At an international storytelling festival held in Singapore, a participant narrated a story that we believe highlights the importance of congruent actions and words.

Singapore Airlines

On 31 October 2000, Singapore Airlines experienced their first fatal air disaster. Singapore Airlines had a perfect safety record and was an iconic company that Singaporeans were proud of. Such was the interest in the company's response that the press conferences were televised live across the country.

Rick Clements was the president of public affairs and during one press conference was saying everything you would expect him to say: that he was sorry this had happened, that they were doing everything they could to help the victims and grieving relatives and that they would review the processes and systems to ensure it never happened again.

At this point, a man who had lost his brother in the crash interrupted the press conference, demanding more information. He was very emotional and angry. A security guard stepped in and tried to take the man away, but Clements waved all the security men away, approached the man and hugged him.

The woman who shared this story said, 'That one action showed us all that they were serious in what they were saying and that they truly cared'. Can you imagine the lack of connection that would have been demonstrated had Clements allowed the security guards to remove the man?

We know it is 'Leadership 101' stuff to say that your words and actions need to be congruent — you have to talk the talk, and walk the walk, and all that stuff — but this becomes crucial when you start sharing stories because your stories will have a greater impact than just your words. They will be remembered and repeated. Don't be scared of this. Embrace it and just make sure your actions and stories are aligned.

How actions create stories

In leadership there are three kinds of stories that emerge:

1 *The stories you tell as a leader.* These are deliberate and strategic.

2 *Your stories repeated by others.* These are the very same stories you tell as a leader. (Before your head gets inflated, note that this does not happen very often.)

3 *The stories told about you.* These are taken from what you have said and done — for example, your actions, words and decisions all generate stories.

Like it or not, your actions generate stories. There are already stories of you out there! People are already sharing stories about you, about your leadership style, about your values and what you are like to work for and work with. Here is an example of how people's actions can create stories about them.

The Cameron Clyne story

In 2008, when Cameron Clyne took over as CEO at National Australia Bank (NAB), one of his early promises was to be open and approachable. When he was still fairly new to the job, he attended one of NAB's internal events and took a seat at the back of the room. A lady who worked in IT approached him and said, 'Excuse me. You are sitting in my seat'. He immediately apologised and vacated her seat.

As soon as Cameron left, one of the lady's colleagues said, 'Do you know who that was? It was the new CEO!' The lady said, 'You're kidding. No way! Why would he sit up the back?' She was extremely embarrassed and copped a friendly ribbing from her peers for quite a while.

That story spread through the bank like wildfire, probably because it was a funny story. What it did, though, was show NAB's employees the congruence between Cameron's words and his actions.

Imagine if Cameron had responded differently by saying, 'Excuse me. Do you know who I am? How dare you ask me to move'. That story would have also spread through NAB and Cameron's credibility around being 'open and approachable' would have been shot to pieces.

A famous example of actions creating stories is the one of ex-Woolworths CEO Roger Corbett. He once found a Woolworths trolley in Sydney's Circular Quay and pushed it 1.5 kilometres to return it to the store. This story has not only become legendary throughout Woolworths, but is often cited as an example of a leader being a role model for his employees and living the values he wants his employees to live.

It is important to understand that your actions will generate stories. As a leader, be aware of this and work with it. Make sure your actions generate positive stories, not negative stories.

In a nutshell

Did you get hooked?

→ Sometimes you may get an immediate 'Wow!' when you tell a story, but usually deferred gratification is more the norm for storytellers.

→ Good stories have a long tail and your story may be repeated or requested six months after you first told it.

→ Check whether your stories worked by gauging audience engagement, looking for a silence after your story (this is a good thing), finding out if your story is repeated by other people and checking your Twitter feed.

→ Get better at storytelling by reflecting on your stories.

→ Use either The Traffic Signal Approach or The Story Impact Matrix as tools for reflection.

→ Reflect as soon as you can after finishing a story. The less time that passes between when you use a story and when you reflect on it, the better your reflection will be.

→ Maximise your return on investment by understanding the six Rs of storytelling: reuse, retire, recycle, reject, replenish and retain.

→ Ensure your stories and actions are congruent.

→ Your actions create words: make sure your actions generate positive stories, not negative stories.

How hooked are you?

→ What measure(s) are you going to use to gauge the success of your stories?

→ Which of the two reflection tools discussed (The Traffic Signal Approach or The Story Impact Matrix) are you going to use to help improve your storytelling skills?

→ Which of the six Rs of storytelling (reuse, retire, recycle, reject, replenish and retain) are you going to implement with your stories?

→ What stories of you are already out there and how can you check that your stories and actions are congruent?

→ Your actions create stories. As a leader, how are you going to make this work for you and not against you?

In this chapter we looked at the secrets of storytelling to help you take your storytelling to the next level. In the next chapter we will explore where you can start sharing your stories.

CHAPTER 8
Getting your stories out there

There is no greater agony than bearing an untold story inside you.

Maya Angelou, American author and poet

A leader who attended one of our workshops said to us afterwards, 'I had 10 meetings this week, and what I realise now is that I had 10 missed opportunities to share stories'. Please don't let that be your fate.

Once you have created your stories, you really need to get out there and start sharing them as a leader within your organisation—share them with your team members, the board, clients and stakeholders. And, guess what? Story opportunities are not going to be presented to you on a silver platter: you have to proactively find and create these opportunities. Your stories will be of no use to anyone locked away in your head.

In this chapter we are going to explore some ways in which you, as an individual, can share stories in various business contexts.

This is all about you getting out there, inspiring and making a difference by using storytelling.

Facts tell — stories sell

The very best salespeople use stories because they understand the powerful role stories play in sales — which is that stories help clients connect emotionally with you and your product. Great salespeople know that people buy on emotion and justify their purchase on logic. They understand that if you are using only facts, figures and product benefits, you are 'telling'. If you are showing the value of these facts, figures and product benefits through stories, you are selling.

Think of the sales pitches you are involved in or have been involved in and then think of where you could use stories. We have seen clients use a story at the very start of a sales conversation to create an instant connection. We have also seen clients provide some data and then successfully segue into stories with, 'For example ...'

People don't really buy a product, service, or idea; they buy the story that's attached to it.

Michael Margolis, *Believe Me: A Storytelling Manifesto for Change-makers and Innovators*

Opportunities to use stories in sales are unlimited and never for a moment will your clients think, 'Ah ha! You just told a story'. Instead, they will feel more connected, engaged and inspired by you, possibly without even realising why.

One of our clients, Matthew, provides products and solutions around effectively using water in remote areas. In his sales process, instead of just listing the features and benefits of his products he shares a customer story of a young farming couple who very cautiously installed his product and how the wife, who was sitting at her kitchen table, rang him excitedly one morning and said, 'Oh my god, you have saved me three hours of driving to start the generator. I just started it from my kitchen table!'

To find stories to use in sales you need to be on the lookout for your customers' stories and you need to ask the right questions to draw out these stories.

So, for example, if your customers say to you, 'This product has changed my life', ask them for a specific example and find out the whole story by asking, 'How has it changed your life?' Start to dig deeper.

This is how you build up your suite of stories. Just as Matthew did, think back on past interactions with customers and what they actually said to you. Or, alternatively, start taking notice of what they say in the future and keep asking them questions until you feel you have a great customer success story.

Once you have these stories, you can use them from your day-to-day conversations with customers or potential customers right through to your formal written proposal, tender or pitch. What if you are not at the coalface and do not have any direct customer or client contact? Then interview or badger someone who does. Ask them lots of questions to elicit examples of how clients engage with your services and products and then use the proven story formula we shared with you in chapter 4 to convert these into stories that you can use.

As a leader, don't think of selling as something you only do in a face-to-face meeting. There is collateral you use on a day-to-day basis that does the job of selling for you — for example, your business cards.

When we had our business cards designed, we decided to challenge ourselves by inserting a mini story on our business cards! Now *that* was hard to do in such a confined space. This is how our business cards read:

- **Gabrielle Dolan** unwittingly started crafting her storytelling skills as a young child growing up with seven brothers and sisters and competing for her parents' attention. You can get her attention by contacting her on ...

- **Yamini Naidu** grew up in Mumbai (Bombay) India where she travelled daily on a red bus to school. To pass time on the journey, she often imagined the bus was a tiger. To hear more stories of travelling by tiger you can contact her on ...

We love our business cards and they are one thing we have not outgrown over our years in business. Our clients also love our business cards and we were even asked to run a workshop on personal branding because one client was impressed by how memorable our business cards were and the impact they had.

So think laterally about where you can use stories in sales.

Social media

Social media and storytelling are like basil and tomatoes: they are meant to be together and bring out the best of each other.

Blogs

If you write a blog, this is a perfect place to share stories. It is also a perfect place for you to start capturing all your stories.

We often refer back to our blog to reference stories that we shared through that medium.

The internet is allowing us to get back to what's really more natural, which is that storytelling is a shared thing. It's our natural way to be communal.

Joseph Gordon-Levitt, American actor and director

You can also use your personal or company Facebook page or LinkedIn page to share stories or to link the stories on your blog or website.

Instead of just making a trite statement in a blog post, see if you can support it with a story. The story helps make your point stick and also makes your blog post interesting and memorable, but you already know that... right?

One example is a blog post by author Peter Guber — who is CEO of Mandalay Entertainment and owner of the Golden State Warriors and the Los Angeles Dodgers — in which he talks about why it is important to lose... a lot.

Guber starts his blog post with a story describing how he was sitting in the floor seats at a Golden State Warriors basketball game at about 9 pm one night. The team was behind by two points in the closing minutes of the game and he grimaced and held his fists to his eyes as one of the key players missed two crucial foul shots in a row.

He then writes, 'Suddenly, I was pinged on my Smartphone and it was Pat Riley, the President of the Miami Heat. He happened to be watching our game from his bedroom at home in Miami around midnight. He exhorted, "Don't do that! Losing is part of the game! Listen to these statistics... you play... for as much as 270 games a year. You are going to lose a lot! A lot! Get used to it!"'

After hooking the reader in with a personal story, Guber then goes on to write about why it is important to lose.

YouTube

YouTube is also a perfect place to record some of your own stories or to get your customers sharing and uploading their stories. Just make sure they are short and sharp.

Twitter

'A 140-character story on Twitter. Is that possible?' we hear you say. Well, it probably is possible, but very hard to do.

Way before Twitter, in the 1920s Ernest Hemingway's colleagues bet that he could not write a complete story in just six words. Hemingway responded with, 'For sale: baby shoes, never used'. Poignant. The colleagues paid up. Hemingway is said to have considered it his best work.

For the rest of us mere mortals a 140-character story continues to pose challenges.

However, you could put the opening line of your story on Twitter and then link it to your post. If it captures your audience, the opening line will leave them wanting more.

Emails

Every time we present on storytelling, someone always asks, 'Can you use stories in emails?' By now you will have guessed that we are story evangelists, so our answer is always, 'Yes, you can! You can use stories in your emails — hallelujah'.

Of course, not in every email; that would be tedious and you would never get any work done. But every time you want to make a point stick or you want to influence behaviour, a story can help.

Jade's organisation was notorious for having leaders who always said they wanted more training, but when a training day was organised they would claim they were too time poor to attend. She had a look at the email communication that went out inviting leaders to training days. Predictably, it was of the most boring variety. The subject headings alone would be enough to entice most people to hit the delete key.

This is how she communicated the next email invitation to the leaders.

Emails and stories

Subject heading: A man was ...

... struggling in the woods to saw down a tree. An old farmer came by, watched for a while, then quietly said, 'What are you doing?'

'Can't you see?' the man replied impatiently, 'I'm sawing down this tree'.

'You look exhausted,' said the farmer. 'How long have you been at it?'

'Over five hours, and I'm beat,' replied the man. 'This is hard work.'

'That saw looks pretty dull,' said the farmer. 'Why don't you take a break for a few minutes and sharpen it? I'm sure it would go a lot faster.'

'I don't have time to sharpen the saw,' the man says emphatically. 'I'm too busy sawing!'

Are you ready to sharpen your saw? Here are the details of our next session ...

The email went on to provide details of the training as well as the attribution for the story (Stephen Covey, *The 7 Habits of Highly Effective People*). Jade's organisation had a 100-per-cent attendance at the next training program. No leader could say they did not have the time to sharpen their saw. This email communication created a connection by using a story that moved people into action...that is the power of a story in an email.

Forget the elevator pitch

How many times have you been asked, 'So, what do you do?' You may have to explain what you do and explain it quickly. Enter the term 'elevator pitch'.

We have never been fans of the elevator pitch. Most elevator pitches are boring. They get you to talk about what you do, where you work and the benefits your services provide. Of course, there are countless varieties of elevator pitch, but they all tend to be pretty bland — for example, 'We provide management consulting services to medium-to-large business across a variety of industries'.

The reality is that describing what you do in the time it takes for an elevator to go up or down is difficult unless you secretly hit the emergency stop button and secure another five or 10 minutes while the engineers getting it going again.

So we think it's time to kill off the elevator pitch once and for all and replace it with a story that describes what you do. It does not have to explain exactly what you do in every situation for every type of customer you have. Often, even though someone has asked you what you do, they are probably not actually very interested at all. They may just be politely initiating small talk.

We are sharing this with you because when you do get asked 'What do you do?', there may be some interest, but it is not an invitation to give a running history on your company or start reeling off your résumé. By all means tell them what you do, but do it in an engaging way.

In 2010 we had the pleasure of doing some pro bono work in the form of a storytelling workshop for Many Rivers. Many Rivers provide micro-financing, predominantly for indigenous Australians. One of the participants was David Bagheri who, as National Development Manager for Many Rivers, was often in a position of explaining what they did. He would have to explain to many of their clients and potential clients that Many Rivers was there to support them, but not to do the work for them. He would also find himself explaining this to others who thought the company was a charity giving away money.

This is the story David developed during our workshop to communicate his message.

The butterfly story

I remember a few years ago watching a documentary on butterflies. They start off as caterpillars and munch and crunch their way through leaves. Eventually they cocoon themselves and then turn into butterflies. What I didn't know, however, was that the process of the butterfly breaking out of the cocoon is quite strenuous and can take a while to do. This long and strenuous process actually strengthens the butterfly's wings. It allows the butterfly to have the strength in its wings to fly away from the cocoon.

If someone decided to help the butterfly while still in its cocoon by removing the layers of the cocoon, the butterfly would be denied the opportunity to strengthen its wings. Once free from the cocoon, the butterfly would fall to the ground and die.

At Many Rivers we provide business guidance and financial support to indigenous start-up companies and individuals, but we would never deny our clients the opportunity to strengthen their wings. Instead, we help them fly like a butterfly.

Consider how refreshing this would be to hear after you have asked someone what they do. Many people have heard us retell David's story. What surprises us is how other people find different applications for that story. We have had teachers use it with their students and parents use it with their children to remind both children and students that the role we play as parents and teachers is to assist them, but not to deny them the opportunity to 'strengthen their wings'.

Stories to the rescue

Stories can be used to convey a multitude of messages in the business environment. They can save you from tricky situations and from having to make awkward decisions, among other things. Here are some examples.

Answering questions

As coaches, consultants or leaders we are often asked questions that we do not have the answers to, or we may want to provide guidance but not a direct answer. This is where a story can help.

Here is an example from one of our clients, Jon Kaehne, who was a consultant at a global consulting firm. Jon was in a meeting where the CEO and the supply chain executive were disputing what the firm's supply chain service levels should be. Should they be 95 per cent? 96 per cent? 97 per cent? Unable to reach an agreement, they turned to Jon and said, 'Jon, you are the expert. What is the correct answer?' Not wanting to take sides or pluck a figure out of thin air, Jon responded with this story.

Jon's Nordstrom story

A few years ago I was in Portland, Oregon and my wife had given me a long shopping list which included a very specific pair of Guess jeans. I was in Nordstrom (a US department store) and, loaded down with shopping bags, I went to the ladies-wear department to look for jeans. The sales assistant said, 'We don't stock Guess jeans, but can I interest you in a pair of Diesel or Lee jeans?' I said they were for my wife and I had specific instructions to purchase that exact pair of Guess jeans. The assistant then said, 'Are you happy to leave your bags here with another staff member and come with me?'

I agreed and she escorted me out of the store and down the street to the Guess store. She introduced me by name to the Guess sales assistant, who found the jeans I was after. I purchased them and then returned with the Nordstrom sales assistant to Nordstrom to get my bags.

What is the relevance of this story? ... Nordstrom's customer service level was 110 per cent. That is the right service level for every firm.

Jon then told us that the CEO just looked at him, hit the table with delight and said, 'That's why I love you guys!'

Coaching

In coaching and mentoring situations, stories can be readily applied. They work in this context as they have the ability to provide subtle advice without being directive.

Christine Nixon, ex-Chief Commissioner of Victoria Police, was very passionate about the importance of setting goals in your professional career and also in your personal life. She would often share a story on the importance of setting goals when she provided coaching.

We have had the pleasure of seeing Christine present many times and of speaking to her about how she has used stories to great effect throughout her career. This is the story (published in her book *Fair Cop*) that she would often tell to share her message about goal setting. It describes her experiences at the FINA World Swimming Championships in 2007. On the first day, as each competing country's name was called out, a float was placed in the pool with the country's flag on it.

Goal setting

There were all these floats just bobbing around the pool, that is all they were doing... just bobbing around.

The next day I went to watch the actual competition... and what a contrast. These athletes were so focused and targeted. They stood at one end of the pool with the sole purpose to win that race. When the starter's gun went they just got to the other end of the pool in the most direct... way they could. I often reflect on... how many of us are just bobbing around with no direction, without a goal...

Christine shared with us that often, after telling that story, people would come up to her and thank her. With tears in their eyes they would say, 'I have just realised I was one of those floats bobbing around... but not any longer'.

When we share this story with others we are amazed of how many people have heard Christine speak and to this day remember that story and others she has told. People not only remember the stories; they also remember the advice packaged in the stories.

Managing employees

During performance management conversations or when you have to give someone really tough feedback, stories are a valuable tool. Stories have the ability to be nonjudgemental. They are like a velvet sledgehammer. They can really ram home a point without the person feeling they have had a point rammed into them.

One example of this involves a client of ours, Sam. Sam managed a team of hedge fund managers.

Sam had a young man in his team who was his best performer. But — and here is the very big but — some of his behaviour was not acceptable. Other members in the team had approached Sam to say that while this individual may hit his targets, he was not a team player; he was rude and selfish and, as one of the team members put it, he was a complete 'a***hole'.

Sam knew he had to do something, but his challenge was to let this guy know that he was being an a***hole without getting his best performer offside.

Sam took the young man out for a coffee and during a conversation about how he was getting on at work, Sam shared the following story with him.

The guy with the iPod

Last month I was waiting for my train and next to me on the platform were an elderly lady, another businessman and a young guy with his iPod earphones in his ears. When the train pulled up, the businessman and I stood back, allowing the elderly lady to enter the train first.

I couldn't believe it when the young guy pushed through the doors, nearly knocking the lady over. With his earphones in his ears and in his rush to get on the train I'm convinced he didn't even know what he'd done.

The other businessman and I looked at each other in disbelief. He then said to me in a loud voice and looking directly at the young guy, 'I always wanted to know what an a***hole looked like and now I do'. With that, the young guy took his earphones out of his ears and asked, in a genuine tone, 'Pardon?' As I had thought, he had no idea what he'd done.

Do you think sometimes we act a bit like that guy with his earphones stuck in his ears — when we're too focused on our targets — and other people might see us as being a***holes?

Sam told us later that he was unsure if the story worked at the time. He said that there was a bit of silence after the story and there certainly was no questioning along the lines of, 'Why are you telling me this?' or 'Are you saying that I'm an a***hole?' But he also said there were no comments such as, 'Yeah, some people can be really rude'.

So Sam was not sure it had worked, but over the next few weeks he said he started to observe some changes in the young man's behaviour (for the better) and subtle differences in how he treated the rest of the team.

The story gave Sam a safe way of addressing his challenge of letting his star performer know his behaviour was unacceptable but still keeping him onside. The story also gave Sam a way of continually managing performance. When he saw the behaviour creeping back in he could ask him — in front of the team — 'Did we just push an old lady over to get on the train?'

We are not going to suggest that it was easy for Sam to come up with that story and to tell it. He spent a lot of time finding the right example and practising to make sure it would work for him.

Presenting

Every time you present, you need stories to help your audience connect with you and connect with your key messages. Think about how you can start with a story or end with a story to ensure your presentation is remembered.

The fine line between speaking and being heard is storytelling.

Greg Power, TEDxVancouver, 2011

The shorter your presentation, the more you need stories. We helped a friend who was entering a competition and only had three minutes to speak to weave in one powerful story. She came running into our office screaming with delight straight after she had won the competition.

A CEO we were working with was presenting at his company's conference on employee engagement. His key message was to get the leaders to start thinking differently about employee engagement. This is the story he told during his presentation.

The money and the chocolates

A boy was walking along the road and a man came up to him in a car and said, 'I will give you $10 and a bar of chocolate to get into the car'. The boy continued walking without looking at the man.

A couple of minutes later the car approached the boy again and the man said, 'Okay, what about if I give you $50 and two bars of chocolate. Will you get into the car then?' The boy continued walking, ignoring the driver.

Another minute passed. The car approached the boy again and this time the man said, 'All right, you win. I will give you $100 and all the chocolate you can eat'. With that the boy stopped, walked over to the car and said, 'Dad, you bought the Volvo. You live with the consequences'.

And that goes to show that it takes more than money and chocolates to motivate people.

The CEO then went on to explain the strategy, the challenges and the opportunities for the next 12 months. But he had clearly identified upfront the most important message he wanted to deliver to his audience — he wanted them to start thinking differently about employee engagement.

An example of someone ending with a story is John Burgin, Vice President of Cognizant. John was hosting an event in July 2012 for his clients and after a day of listening to speeches by keynote speakers he wanted to leave them with one message. The message was that it was now up to them to decide what to do with the new information and insights. John then ended with the following story.

The wise old man

High in the Himalayan mountains lived a wise old man. Periodically, he ventured down into the local village to entertain the villagers with his special knowledge and talents. One of his skills was to 'psychically' tell the villagers the contents in their pockets, boxes or minds.

A few young boys from the village decided to play a joke on the wise old man to discredit his special abilities. One boy came up with the idea of capturing a bird and hiding it in his hands. He knew, of course, the wise old man would know the object in his hands was a bird, but the boy had devised a plan.

Knowing the wise old man would correctly say the object in his hands was a bird, the boy would ask him if the bird was dead or alive. If the wise old man said the bird was alive, the boy would crush the bird in his hands so that when he opened his hands the bird would be dead; if the wise old man said the bird was dead, the boy would open his hands and let the bird fly free. So, no matter what the old man said, the boy would prove the old man a fraud.

The following week, the wise old man came down from the mountain into the village. The boy quickly caught a bird and, cupping it out of sight in his hands, walked up to the wise old man and asked, 'Old man, old man, what is it that I have in my hands?'

The wise old man said, 'You have a bird'. And he was right.

The boy then asked, 'Old man, old man, tell me, is the bird alive or is it dead?'

The wise old man looked at the boy and said, 'The bird is as you choose it'.

And so it is with what we have learned today. The choice is now yours on how you use the information and if appropriate Cognizant would be honoured to continue to partner you along the way.

So when it comes to your presentations, consider how you can use stories to start and/or end your presentations and how you can use them to get across your key message.

John was a star student of ours. He was not only open to our coaching advice, but readily took our ideas on board. The day of the Cognizant conference he woke up with laryngitis and found it extremely difficult to talk. Soldiering on, he used a story to open the day as well as the one he told to close the day. He had never done that before when presenting. After the event I was talking to one of his team and she said, 'I have seen John present many times and today was the very best I have ever seen him'. The power of storytelling... it can even overcome the enormous challenge of laryngitis!

Remember that stories help people understand and remember your messages. They also inspire people to take action. So, seriously, why would you not use them in your presentations? (That was a rhetorical question — no need to answer!)

Nailing that promotion

Many organisations and individuals either knowingly or unknowingly adopt the Behavioural Event Interviewing (BEI) technique. BEI is a process of asking for specific examples to determine if an applicant has the necessary skills, traits or values for the position being filled.

When asked for specific examples during an interview process, ensure you have a suite of stories available that you have prepared and practised.

The highest paid person in the first half of this century will be the storyteller.

Rolf Jensen, former Director of the Copenhagen Institute for Future Studies

It is not difficult to determine what your interviewee will be looking for. The required skills and desired values will be in the job description of the advertisement.

If the position requires you to be independent and a team player, then have a story prepared that shows how you have displayed both of these skills — or two stories: one for each skill.

For example, imagine if you were asked in a job interview, 'How do you handle the mundane aspects of a job?' You could respond with, 'I appreciate that every job has mundane aspects to it so I just get on with doing what has to be done'. Or you could respond with this.

Piano practice

When I was at school I learned to play the piano. While I enjoyed it, I didn't like the concept of practising the same song and notes over and over again. Even though I knew the practice was important, it became quite boring for me and I really started to lose interest.

One day my piano teacher advised us that we were invited to play at the Sydney Opera House. I was so excited and with this higher objective, I started to practise with a lot more commitment and dedication.

I have experienced this same feeling throughout my career and think back to my piano-playing days. I am prepared to undertake all aspects of the role, even the mundane aspects, when I can see the higher purpose, and when that happens I undertake them with a lot more passion and commitment.

Always have a story ready for when things do not go to plan or when you have failed at something. No-one expects people to be perfect. Displaying vulnerability and admitting mistakes can go a long way. Your stories about how you recovered from these situations or how you dealt with them, can leave a lasting positive impression.

It may be a good idea to test your stories out with a trusted adviser. Sometimes you may prepare a story that you believe demonstrates a particular value, when in fact it may demonstrate a different and perhaps even negative value. You may still be able to use the story, but you may need to change some wording, omit some detail or add detail to ensure the story has its desired result.

You do not need to have a story for every interview question, but you should have a few up your sleeve and aim to have a variety of stories. For example, make sure not all your stories are about the one project or from the one employer. Do not be afraid to bring in personal stories to demonstrate values such as integrity or problem solving.

In a nutshell

Did you get hooked?
→ Once you have created your stories you need to get out there and start sharing them as a leader.

→ Sales, social media, being asked, 'So, what do you do?', answering questions, coaching, managing employees, presenting and nailing that promotion are all opportunities to use storytelling.

How hooked are you?
What stories could you use:

→ when selling/pitching to clients

→ in social media (blogging, tweeting)

→ when you are asked, 'So, what do you do'

→ when answering questions

→ when coaching

→ when performance managing

→ when presenting

→ when nailing that promotion?

In this chapter we looked at the various situations in which you can start using your own stories. In the next chapter we will look at how you can start implementing storytelling across your company.

CHAPTER 9

Implementing storytelling into your organisation

As I look around me today, I see that too few business leaders grasp the idea that stories can have a profound effect on people. The gestures made (or not made) by leaders can turn into the stories that powerfully affect behaviour.

Leaders who understand this and use this knowledge to help make their organisations great are the ones we admire and wish others would emulate. Those in leadership positions who fail to grasp or use the power of stories risk failure for their companies and for themselves.

John Kotter, expert and author on leadership and change

By now you have hopefully realised just how powerful business storytelling is. It can increase your sales, engage your team in a new strategy and make your team meetings more interesting. Now imagine the benefits your organisation would enjoy if everyone in it used storytelling.

To reap the benefits of implementing storytelling into your organisation, you have to take a strategic and sustainable approach. 'Strategic, sustainable storytelling' — try saying that with a lisp!

So what do we mean by 'strategic, sustainable storytelling'?

'Strategic' is trying to understand what you want to achieve by introducing storytelling into your organisation. For example, is it about distinguishing yourself from your competitors; improving your leaders' ability to connect, engage and inspire; or achieving cultural change?

'Sustainable' is about ensuring storytelling becomes your way of doing business and is not just a passing fad.

Strategic, sustainable storytelling includes skilling the relevant people in your organisation on how to use stories, how to proactively find stories, how to choose the right stories to share and how to share these stories across a variety of mediums. It also includes thinking about how you can use stories across a variety of organisational initiatives such as values rollouts or your annual conference.

In this chapter we are going to look at how you can implement storytelling into your organisation. We will also share examples of how organisations have implemented storytelling and how they have used storytelling in organisational initiatives.

Show me how to fish

You may have heard the ancient Chinese proverb, 'Give a man a fish and you feed him for a day. Teach him how to fish and you feed him for a lifetime'. The same wisdom applies to storytelling. It is not enough to tell people to start using stories or give them stories to tell; they have to be shown how to tell stories.

We have both spent a serious chunk of our respective careers in training and leadership roles and have always held strong to the belief that if companies ask their employees to do something, they have a moral obligation to ensure those employees have the skills, confidence and support to undertake what has been asked of them. If you feel 'moral obligation' is a bit righteous, think of it in a practical, logical sense. If you wanted your kid to play the piano, you would enrol them in piano lessons ... right?

If you asked your employees to submit Excel spreadsheets at the end of the month, you would provide them with some training in Excel. If you asked your employees to present at the yearly conference, you would give them some presentation training.

It is the same with storytelling. If you want your employees to start using stories and sharing them throughout your organisation, you need to provide the training and support for them to do that. Otherwise you are going to spend a lot of time listening to some shocking Mozart renditions.

> *Because there is a natural storytelling urge and ability in all human beings, even just a little nurturing of this impulse can bring about astonishing and delightful results.*
>
> **Nancy Mellon,** *The Art of Storytelling*

Skilling of employees is crucial and you have probably realised by now that it is not as easy as just telling them to start using stories.

Cindy Batchelor, a senior leader who saw the need for her top 100 leaders to be given the opportunity to develop their skills in storytelling, agrees. Cindy surmises that 'We give our leaders accountability and responsibility and when we do that we need to build their skills, confidence and capability'.

Cindy went on to explain that senior management knew their leaders were highly technical, highly effective and highly skilled, but that there was a gap in the way they engaged with employees. 'We knew there was a gap so we had the responsibility of fixing it once we had asked them to be responsible and accountable for employee engagement.'

As with any major change, we suggest focusing on the key influencers first. Introducing storytelling into your organisation takes time, money, effort and discipline. It is important for key influencers and senior people to fully understand its power and to experience its power first-hand so they have the motivation to make it happen.

Normally these key influencers are the senior leadership team, but they are not always constrained to just this team. They may also include other key influencers in the business.

You should include supporters of storytelling as well as some of your sceptics. As with any change, it is important to include your sceptics and get them on board early.

Checklist for introducing storytelling

Here's a checklist for introducing storytelling into your organisation.

☑ Introduce storytelling attached to a current business issue, such as low employee engagement, or a way of communicating a new strategy.

☑ Provide leaders and all other relevant employees with training so they can apply storytelling skilfully.

☑ Ensure the senior leadership team is trained early and start role modelling the use of storytelling.

☑ Give leaders the opportunity to practise their stories and to obtain feedback.

☑ Create a culture that supports the use of storytelling.

☑ Develop formal and informal strategies for story sharing among leaders.

☑ Use a structured approach to capture the existing stories within your organisation.

☑ Start sharing stories across your current channels of communication.

So remember, skilling both leaders and employees in storytelling is the crucial first step in implementing strategic, sustainable storytelling.

Finding other people's stories

The first step is always to train leaders in storytelling, as we have discussed. Once everyone is trained, the next challenge is working out how to continually get new stories for leaders to share.

This is where you have to go out into the organisation to find stories about your employees and clients. There are two ways you can proactively find these stories. One way is what we call story harvesting. The other way is to proactively and consciously listen to stories.

Story harvesting works best when used around a topic such as customer service.

Story harvesting

Story harvesting is a process of finding examples of your topic — customer service in this instance; selecting which examples can be crafted into stories; crafting the stories; and deciding why, when and where each story should be shared. It is like digging for gold: you will get a better result if you know where to dig and if you know the difference between real gold and fool's gold.

Story harvesting sessions takes the form of short sessions with a small group (90 to 120 minutes with 10 to 12 people) and skilled storytelling facilitators. Story harvesting sessions need to be carefully planned and expertly facilitated. Both of these points cannot be stressed enough. The planning involves ensuring you have the right people in the room and formulating carefully constructed questions that uncover the right stories.

What do we mean by that? Surely you can just ask people to share stories about customer service or innovation … right? *Wrong.* What we have found is that when you ask someone to tell a story the normal response is, 'I don't have a story'. It puts them under too much pressure as they think it has to be bigger than Ben Hur. It is similar to asking someone to tell you a really funny joke. Their normal reaction would be, 'I don't know a really funny joke'. You need to frame the questions in a way that elicits stories naturally and — this is the tricky bit — without actually ever using the word 'story' in your question.

These story-harvesting sessions begin with the facilitator sharing some appropriate stories and then providing some well-worded questions to uncover more stories. For example:

- 'Share a time when you felt proud to work here.'

- 'Describe a time when you or someone you know at work did the right thing by a customer.'

It is always a good idea to schedule more time than you think you will need as you will be surprised how many stories emerge after the official session has ended.

The facilitator needs to know when to dive deep to uncover the real story. Follow-up questions asked at the appropriate time are important. For example:

- 'How did you feel when that happened?'

- 'What did the customer actually say?'

- 'Describe what you were going through when that happened.'

It is normally after these questions are asked that the real stories emerge.

Once you have uncovered potential examples to craft into stories, you then have to select the stories to use. Which ones you choose will depend on your purpose, but there are a few things to consider when selecting your stories.

First of all, ask the participants in the story-harvesting session two questions:

- Which story did you like best?
- Which story would you be most likely to share with others?

This will give you a really good indication of the 'stickability' of the stories. By 'stickability' we mean the stories people enjoy, remember and are likely to repeat.

Another factor in deciding which stories to select is variety. You will need a good mix of stories across departments and locations and a good variety of stories based on magnitude of impact. Stories that made a difference to one person and a major initiative that had a significant impact on thousands of people are examples of magnitude.

Once the examples are selected, you will need to run them through the proven story formula we shared with you in chapter 4 to turn them into effective business stories. These should then be recorded in a written format. Writing the stories down serves two purposes: it allows you to polish them so they are as effective as they can be; and it gives you a portable piece of communication that can be used in any of your communication channels, such as newsletters, websites and emails. You may want to play with the ending, remove any unwanted detail or add more emotive words.

The final step is working out which stories to share with which audience over which mediums. Depending on your organisation, this will vary. We find this step works best by involving your internal communication professionals, who will be able to guide you.

In March 2012 we conducted some story-harvesting sessions with employees from the call centres, retail branches and other customer-facing areas of a large retail organisation. The company wanted to find stories that would make their employees feel proud to work there.

Here are a couple of the stories that emerged from those sessions. The first one is about Ben, who worked in a call centre.

Ben's story

Upon ending a regular call with, 'Is there anything else I can help you with today?' Ben had the customer break down on the phone as she talked about her current battle with cancer. Ben listened and treated the person with respect and compassion. He asked if there was someone there with her, or someone she could contact. He ended the call by saying that his prayers and thoughts were with her and he hoped everything worked out. What Ben did was not driven by average call times; it did not follow process and procedure. Ben was praised by his team leader because what Ben did was the right thing to do.

This was another story, shared by Ross.

The buddy program

I do a lot of volunteer work with Anglicare. One such initiative is the Buddy Quest program, where a group of men provide positive role modelling to young boys because, for one reason or another, these boys do not have a strong positive male influence in their lives.

One weekend a group of us went trekking and one of the boys fell and really hurt his arm. I did not know it at the time, but he had broken his arm in two places. I walked the rest of the way with him at the back of the pack so we could just keep our own steady pace. There is no doubt I helped him — but he really helped me. You see, I have a sight impairment and I need help to avoid stepping into pot holes or tripping over branches. This young man did that. We walked, we talked and he never once complained about the pain in his arm. I was so proud of him and so glad that our company allows us to have these opportunities.

These stories and the others uncovered in the story-harvesting sessions were then used over a variety of mediums to continually communicate why people valued working for that organisation and they served as a catalyst for others to share similar stories. The story-harvesting sessions are all about proactively searching through your organisation for positive stories that can be shared.

Story harvesting is a formal, structured process for finding stories. While this process gives you great results and allows you to uncover stories you would not normally find, this formal process is not the only way to find stories.

Story listening

The other way of proactively finding stories is by 'story listening' — that is, by asking questions and listening.

To be a good storyteller you need to be a great story listener.

As a leader, you need to get into the habit of asking appropriate questions. Ask questions that may elicit a story and then listen to the answers. If you do hear a story worth sharing further, ask the person if you may use it.

When you are on the hunt for stories, it is best to avoid asking people to tell you a story, but rather to ask them to share an example or an experience.

We heard from one of our clients that when their new general manager met people in the lift he would ask them, 'So, what's your story?' *Gulp* — that's a sure-fire way to kill any conversation! Most people feel cornered, mutter 'hum ha' and then dash out of the lift at the next floor, whether it's their stop or not.

Our experience indicates that if you ask people, 'Tell me a story about great customer service', you will receive a 'no stories here' look. What you need to do is ask for specific examples of customer service … or making a difference … or teamwork … or whatever your topic is.

As a leader you can question individuals, or you can make finding stories part of your team meetings. It can even go on the agenda — but you should call the agenda item an example (not a story).

At Shell Australia the weekly safety meetings start with an agenda item listed as 'Safety share'. This is where all meeting participants share an example or experience about safety from that week.

If you want stories about good customer service, start by asking for examples in your team meetings. You could ask, 'Can anyone share an example of good customer service from this week?' Be prepared to not receive any examples the first time or even the first couple of times. This is normal as people may think you expect an outstanding, amazing example of customer service. But as your team starts to share everyday examples of customer service, this will spark other examples. Be persistent and you will gradually start to hear stories that you can share.

During an interview, Garry Caldow, Strategic Initiatives Manager at Colonial First State Custom Solutions, offered this insight into listening for stories.

'I have found that if you just listen to people and keep your ears open you will hear good stories. You don't need to think of all the stories yourself, but rather when you're listening to someone else's stories think about what that means to you. What you take out of it can then become your story.'

The Power of One

Regardless of how you find your stories — accidentally, by asking questions or through a formal story-harvesting session — you then have to do something with them. Obviously, as an individual you can start to share them across the variety of mediums we discussed in chapter 8: sales meetings, team meetings, presentations, and so on.

In addition to that, as a CEO or senior leader you can also do what we call The Power of One. Upon hearing a story as a senior leader in your organisation, you should make an effort to call, email or visit the person whose story you just heard and congratulate them. For example, if you have a company value of outstanding customer service and you hear a story about an employee delivering amazing customer service, contact them, explain to them that you heard what they did and express to them that this is the exact behaviour and attitude you value as an organisation.

'I don't have time for that,' you may be thinking. 'It's a lot of effort for one person, and I have thousands of employees in my organisation.' These are very valid reactions, but let us ask you this: if you are sitting in a call centre, or in a retail branch, or on a project and you get a call from the CEO thanking you for what you did for the organisation last week or last month, what would you do? You would immediately tell everyone around you and they would tell many more people. They would certainly ask why the CEO called. Your single action will have a ripple effect throughout the organisation. That's The Power of One.

If you are not the CEO or a senior leader but are in a position of influence to get them to take this on board, please encourage them to do so.

The Power of One is the storytelling version of 'catching people doing the right thing, and letting them know you know'. It is simple, yet powerful.

Organisational change

For organisations about to embark on an organisational change — whether it is implementing a new strategy, embarking on significant cultural transformations or instigating a major technical change — the use of storytelling could be significant in ensuring the success of that change.

> *People don't believe what you tell them. They rarely believe what you show them. They often believe what their friends tell them. They always believe what they tell themselves. What leaders do: they give people stories they can tell themselves. Stories about the future and about change.*

Seth Godin, entrepreneur and author

In 2009 we had the privilege of working with the leaders at Ericsson, helping them use and embed storytelling as part of a significant strategic change, which produced measurable positive results. We are going to share a case study of Ericsson Australia and New Zealand to show you just how storytelling can do this.

Case study: Ericsson

This Ericsson case study provides some valuable learnings and insights for leaders who are about to embark on organisational change.

The catalyst

At the start of 2009, Ericsson Australia and New Zealand (the largest global provider of technology services to telecom operators) was facing some tough times. Like many companies during and after the global financial crisis, Ericsson had to find cost savings, and plenty of them. Internally, redundancies were announced, followed by a salary freeze. Externally, customer satisfaction had dropped and competitors were closing the gap at a rapid pace.

The annual internal employee survey results showed that their senior leaders were extremely demotivated as a group, rating only 52 per cent on the motivation index — a worrying result for a group of people whose role it was to motivate and lead others.

Across the entire Australia and New Zealand organisation, the overall motivation score was only 51 per cent. The employees rated their senior leaders only 57 per cent for clear and effective communication. This was significantly below the Ericsson Group rating of 73 per cent.

The process

Sonia Aplin, Head of Communications, stated, 'The challenge for Ericsson Australia and New Zealand was clear, but it was going to require considerable investment and commitment. This was the time for bold action, courage and giant leaps forward. We needed to motivate and engage our leaders and our employees so that they performed better in order to improve our relationship with our customers and, most importantly, strengthen our financial position'.

CEO Jacqueline Hey and the Executive Leadership Team developed and launched a three-year strategy that they hoped would address their particular business challenges and maximise opportunities. A key pillar of the strategy involved transforming the organisation's culture so that it became more customer centric.

They knew they had a good strategy, but they also knew it would account for nothing if they did not build the communication capability of their senior leaders. They understood that it was the leaders who would get people engaged and excited in the strategy on a daily basis ... or not.

The communication team, led by Sonia Aplin, established an official senior leadership team comprising 75 leaders. They then introduced monthly financial updates and quarterly forums for this team as well as an online collaborative site.

Sonia says, 'With some of these hygiene factors of information dissemination in place, it was time to tackle the issue of the communication abilities of this group. I needed something innovative that would not only appeal to our leaders, but would also make a sustainable difference.

'As a communication specialist I'd become fascinated by the way in which US President Barack Obama used stories in his public addresses. Putting politics aside for a moment, it was easy to admire how effectively he used stories to influence people and build his persona. So one day I literally found myself typing "organisational storytelling" into Google — which led to discussions with specialist providers of leadership storytelling training.'

Sonia initially gained support for storytelling from her direct manager and then went about strategically building partners for the concept with the heads of finance, human resources and organisational development.

The storytelling training of the entire 75 leaders was linked to the new strategy program, which was aimed at equipping the leaders with the skills and confidence to communicate with and excite their team regarding the new strategy.

A follow-up survey after the training showed that 98 per cent of this group felt storytelling was a relevant skill to their role as a leader and that they felt it would improve their effectiveness as a leader.

Sonia summarised the training like this:

'The training program itself took our leaders on a journey to show what storytelling is (and what it isn't); evidence of how it helps leaders better engage with their people; why it's important to connect, rather than just communicate; and how stories can drive positive performance and behaviour.

'The program also helped leaders clarify what their specific business challenges were. While all the leaders were coming together to address the overall challenge of transforming our organisation's culture to be more customer centric, each of them had unique challenges that they needed to address with their teams to support the culture change.

'The training included a skilling process to help the leaders develop stories and a session in which the leaders shared their stories for their peers to critique and advise them on. The peer group part of the training was very powerful and kept the leaders committed and on track. An unplanned outcome of the training was the increase in collaboration we saw among the senior leaders as they worked together to test out their stories.'

The results

As soon as the training commenced, there was an instant increase in the use of stories around the organisation, as well as at conferences and customer presentations. Previously the leaders had been very serious and impersonal and now they were starting to share stories about their previous work and other life experiences. Naturally, all these stories were aligned with their business purpose.

Skilling up all the leaders in a relatively short time (over three months) resulted in the leaders supporting each other in the use of stories, and a group commitment to starting to use stories, which initiated the very important role-model process.

The incoming CEO, Jacqueline Hey, who had inherited poor customer and employee satisfaction results, launched the company's Customer Centric culture program with this story.

> I recently visited the Auckland office where the country manager, Jeff, asked me if I'd flown with the airline Pacific Blue. I said, 'Yes, they were great'. Jeff said, 'Really? You didn't find space to be an issue?'

And actually he was right, because when the guy sitting in front of me reclined his seat there was no room for me to open my laptop. And when I thought about the experience a bit more I thought of the sandwich which I'd bought that had been a bit stale. So why did I feel so good about the flight? It was because from the moment I checked in until the moment I left the plane the Pacific Blue staff were friendly, attentive and they showed great passion for what they did.

At Ericsson, we focus on getting our technology perfect when in fact it's the way we interact with our customers which makes all the difference.

The figures

By the end of 2009, after the storytelling training had been completed, there had been some significant improvements at Ericsson. The employee survey results showed that the leadership communication index increased from 57 to 75 per cent — a massive 18-per-cent increase. Strategy awareness increased by 11 per cent and motivation increased by 8 per cent. Motivation for the senior leadership group also increased by a staggering 22 per cent.

In addition, customers rated Ericsson 5 per cent ahead of their competitors and they finished the year in a much stronger financial position.

Sonia states, 'These successes were of course due to a range of initiatives that we introduced as an organisation but certainly, equipping our leaders to be more effective communicators was a key contributor to these results'.

Ericsson then identified other employees who would benefit from being equipped with storytelling skills, such as their salespeople.

Lessons learnt

There were several lessons learnt during this process. Sonia Aplin states her three key learnings as:

'The first is the importance of partnering both internally and externally. The partnership between the communication and HR departments helped to get the program off the ground. In addition, the expertise of the external training providers ensured that once the program was up and running, it was well received by our leaders.

'The second lesson for me as a professional communicator was how critical it is to align with the business strategy if you are to attract senior leadership buy-in. As communication specialists we inherently see the value of learning a new skill such as organisational storytelling, but understandably, the value is not immediately seen by our colleagues. Attaching communication initiatives to a business program helps fast track buy-in from other areas of the company.

'Finally, I learned a lesson in how powerful the peer group can be when I saw the leaders both support and influence each other to take full advantage of the training.'

For Ericsson and organisations embarking on an organisational change, the use of storytelling is significant in ensuring the success of that change.

Communicating values

Have you ever lived through a values rollout? Are there any two other words in the English language that make you conjure up images of sophisticated graphic models and mouse pads as much as 'values rollout'? Most people who worked in business in the 1990s were subject to quite a few values rollouts, which bred a healthy level of cynicism.

Values rollouts — where companies come up with a 'unique' set of values such as teamwork, integrity and customer service and then communicate these values to their employees — were done so badly for so long, they rightly gained a bad reputation. In fact, they gained such a bad reputation that some organisations re-labelled their values as corporate principles.

Regardless of how values evolve, we want to pose a question: How do you get your people to understand your corporate values or principles without stories? Think about that, and if you know of another way we would love to hear about it.

We believe that only through stories can you bring real understanding to what you mean by each of the values and behaviours.

Let's look at one of the most common values that nearly every organisation would espouse: outstanding customer service. It is a value that is often stated, but does it really make a difference? For example, do any of your competitors have a stated value of 'pretty average customer service'?

An example of an organisation that has successfully rolled out its value of outstanding customer service is Nordstrom. You will remember Jon's fantastic experience at Nordstrom in Oregon, which we described in chapter 8.

Nordstrom is an American retail store known for its outstanding customer service. What sets Nordstrom apart is that it does not consider customer service a strategy, but rather a way of life. Nordstrom continually reinforces this by sharing stories of customer service that are above and beyond the call of duty. In the Nordstrom culture, these stories are called 'heroics'.

One such story is about a man who sent a letter to Nordstrom that described his difficulty in getting a suit he bought there to fit, despite several visits for alterations. When CEO John Nordstrom heard about the complaint, he organised a new suit to be delivered to the customer, along with a Nordstrom tailor to make sure the jacket and pants fit perfectly. When the alterations were completed, the suit was delivered free of charge.

Then there is the story of a customer who fell in love with a pair of burgundy, pleated Donna Karan slacks that had just gone on sale at the Nordstrom store in Seattle. The store was out of her size, and the sales assistant was unable to track down a pair at any of the five other Nordstrom stores in the Seattle area. Aware that the same slacks were available across the street at a competitor's store, the associate secured some petty cash from her department manager and went across the street to the rival department store, where she bought the slacks (at full price), returned to Nordstrom and then sold them to the customer for the marked-down Nordstrom price. Obviously, Nordstrom did not make money on that sale, but it was an investment in promoting the loyalty of an appreciative customer, who more than likely thought of Nordstrom when planning her next purchase.

As such stories spread throughout an organisation, employees soon see that the people who run the company recognise and reward outstanding acts of customer service. They discover that management is not just giving lip service to customer service, but actually doing something about it.

Through the stories they also get to fully understand the 'outstanding' in 'outstanding customer service' and are empowered by way of the stories to do whatever it takes to deliver this customer service.

When we share these stories with clients who also have an 'outstanding customer service' value they often respond with, 'We don't do that' or, 'We would not do that'. If that is the case, the value of 'outstanding customer service' is only an espoused value and not a value in action.

Another example of a story that demonstrates a value comes from a senior leader, Matt Ricker. He shared a powerful story that has gained a life of its own throughout his organisation. This is Matt's story (overleaf).

> **Make our nanas proud**
>
> Twenty years ago when I got my job with a bank I rushed home to tell my family. I was so excited. I remember my nana saying to me, 'That's great because if you work hard, one day you will become a bank manager and they really mean something in society'. When I reflect back on the past 20 years of my career in the banking industry, I don't think there are too many nanas out there who are proud of their grandchildren working for a bank. What I hope to achieve with our new strategy is to make sure there are a lot of nanas out there who are proud of their grandkids for working for NAB.

We can't imagine how any organisation can hope to have a successful values rollout without using stories. The Nordstrom example is a case in point. If your organisation lives and breathes its values there should be stories to support that. Find those stories and share them widely to make your organisation's values come alive.

Your next event

Conferences and leadership summits are perfect opportunities for sharing stories. In September 2012, we worked with a large department in a global organisation to assist them with their leadership conference. As well as presenting all the information on what had been achieved to date and the targets for next year, the conference organisers also wanted to reinforce the values of the organisation.

They selected four first-year graduates to reflect on their experiences over the year. The graduates did this by sharing a short story each. The graduates and the stories were selected to ensure variety. One was on customer service, one focused on professional development opportunities, another focused on volunteering opportunities and the fourth on the support and coaching that leaders provided.

The four graduates sat on stools up on stage. One graduate would share their story, then pause; then the next graduate would share their story, and so on. One of the graduates was Mitchell. Here is his story.

Mitchell's story

It was March 2010 and I was in my final year at university. Graduate positions had begun opening and I quickly realised I had no idea what I wanted to do next year. I decided to apply for any graduate program I was even remotely qualified for. After learning about organisations and attending a few interviews I kept getting the impression most organisations wanted to know what I could do for them. One company I spoke to wanted to know what we could do together. I really liked that.

With that company, I got to the group interview phase and the graduate management team began by giving an amazing overview of the company, the culture and most importantly their volunteering program, which I had never heard about. Honestly, it sounded too good to be true and I had already heard a few sales pitches from other organisations.

I went away and did my research by speaking to previous graduates and employees. I spoke to my friend Ben who worked here and he repeated the graduate team's message, telling me how great the culture really was. He sounded like he was in love.

A year later I began working here and decided to start testing my newfound relationship ... I took advantage of the graduate

(continued)

Mitchell's story (cont'd)

title and went up to a huge variety of people asking them to take time out and have a coffee with me. Not a single person ever said no.

I decided it was time to test volunteering, something I am really passionate about. I spoke with my team and without any effort they were on board. We are now set to go and work with Save the Children helping define their strategic direction.

It turns out our company walks the walk and, just like Ben, I too love working here.

All the four graduates did was share their stories — nothing more. But they did this after appropriate training and practice. It took no longer than eight minutes from start to end and was the most powerful eight minutes of the entire conference. A lot of the executives in the room that day had tears of joy and pride in their eyes.

What was vital to the effectiveness of this was that the graduates moved away from what people would traditionally do at annual meetings and instead introduced themselves and explained what they were about to do. For example, 'Hi, my name is Mark and I am going to share with you a story about my first year of working here'. Sometimes all you need to do is tell the story. Nothing beforehand and only a pause and applause afterwards.

We adopted a similar approach when working in Melbourne with Flemington Primary School's grade 6 graduation. It was traditional that the 12 school leaders all gave a short speech.

Instead, the 12 leaders stood on stage and each of them shared a one-minute story from their primary-school years. There were stories about friendship, stories about teachers, stories from the first day of school, stories from camps and stories about sporting days. Stories reflected the values of the school.

Here is an example from Ella.

Ella's story

I love school, and I am really going to miss everything and everyone next year. All of my strongest memories are from the amazing friends I have made and the great teachers I've had.

There is one thing in particular that makes me laugh every time I think about it and it's about one of my teachers, Phil.

It was one lunchtime earlier this year and Audrey, Sophie, Mia in grade 2 and I were sitting on the green bench beside the oval, just chatting away, talking about girl stuff, as we do. Phil just happened to be on yard duty and he comes over to us and says, 'How are you going, girls? Chatting about girl stuff?' And all of a sudden he starts singing, 'All the single ladies, all the single ladies' and doing the Beyoncé dance moves. I just thought how cool it was that my teacher can do daggy dad dancing and not be embarrassed! I mean, there were quite a few people watching and he was singing it pretty loud. I just thought it was hilarious. And now every time we sit in that spot and he's on duty, he comes over and sings that song.

Memories like this will stay with me forever and remind me how much I loved Flemington Primary School.

Here is a story from Sophie.

Sophie's story

I remember in grade 6 at the interschool swimming sports I was nearing the end of a long day at Queens Park pool when my butterfly race was just about to start. I had been training for weeks, so the coldness and length of the pool were normal to me. But there was one thing that was different from my training. Every single time I came up for a breath, all that I could hear was the kids from Flemington shouting out encouragements and praise. Silence — screaming, silence — screaming, for the entire race. They never gave up, not even for a second. And when I finished the race and looked back at them, everyone had a huge smile on their face, like I had just won a gold medal at the Olympics.

Out of all my seven fantastic years in primary school, this was the moment that most reminded me, and will remind me for the rest of my life, how much I love and will miss being a Flemington Primary School student.

These stories were delivered in isolation. One child would share their story, then there would be a pause, followed by applause from the crowd before the next story was shared.

This entire process took no longer than 15 minutes and was an amazing walk down memory lane for students, teachers and parents. The students' delivery of these stories was a highlight for parents and teachers.

No matter what kind of event you are running at work, or even in your local primary school, there is power in having people share their stories to create an unforgettable experience for your audience.

In a nutshell

Did you get hooked?

→ Once your leaders are trained in storytelling the next challenge is working out how to get new stories for leaders to share using either story harvesting or story listening.

→ On hearing a story about an employee, senior leaders in your organisation should ring, email or visit the person whose story they just heard and congratulate them. This is The Power of One and it has a huge ripple effect.

→ For organisations embarking on organisational change, the use of storytelling could be significant in ensuring the success of that change.

→ Values rollout and storytelling go hand in hand: you cannot hope to have a successful values rollout without the use of storytelling.

→ Consider getting people to share their stories (after suitable skilling and training) at your next event or leaders' summit.

How hooked are you?

→ Consider who in your company could benefit from learning the skill of storytelling and invest in them to help them develop this skill.

→ Do you have stories hidden away in your company that very few people know about? If so, consider conducting story-harvesting sessions to uncover these stories.

→ If you are in a position to implement The Power of One, start immediately. This is a simple, easy initiative that can have amazing results.

→ Consider other applications of storytelling in your company such as the communication of your values or your next big event.

In this chapter we explored how you can start implementing storytelling into your company. Now we hand it over to you and hope that you will give it a go!

CHAPTER 10

Giving it a go

If it doesn't challenge you it won't change you.

**Brent Lavery, Owner and Manager,
Paramount Health and Fitness**

So where to now? What brave new steps are you going to take as a result of buying and reading this book?

There is a wonderful scene from the movie *Indiana Jones and the Last Crusade* in which Sean Connery plays Indy's father, Dr Henry Jones.

Although his father is dying, Indiana has to continue on the crusade for the Holy Grail. Indiana comes across a large ravine that is impossible to cross. He reads the ancient instructions, which say, 'Only in the leap from the lion's head will he prove his worth'... and he realises he needs to take a leap of faith. His dying father mutters, 'You must believe, boy' and with that Indy takes the successful leap of faith, crossing to the other side of the ravine on a previously hidden bridge.

So now we ask you to do one thing and one thing only. No, we are not asking you to step into a ravine to certain death — we are asking you take a leap of faith. Although you have worked hard to learn all about storytelling, from our own experience and that of all our clients we know it is perfectly natural and normal to feel a certain amount of trepidation.

So we invite you to take a leap of faith and also want to assure you that while we ask you to take a leap of faith with us it is a tiny little leap of faith. It is normal to feel anxious, but that is no excuse to not do it. As Dr Henry Jones says, 'You have to believe'. So believe in the power of storytelling.

Can you remember Liza Boston's story from chapter 4, and the success she experienced when skiing down Mount Hutt? She shared with us that before she launched into her story she was really hesitant and thought, 'leap of faith, leap of faith' and just did it. She also admitted later to us that she was more scared of coming back and telling us she did not have the courage to tell the story than she was of actually saying it.

We would like to end with just one message: make a start by sharing just one of the stories you have so carefully crafted, practised and polished. When you are about to share your story and if you are feeling a bit anxious, acknowledge that feeling, accept that it is normal and be like Indiana Jones: take that leap of faith. As a leader you have no other choice.

Go out and connect, engage and inspire. Get people hooked on you and your messages. As a leader, you now have the most powerful means to do that.

STORY INDEX

INDEX

We would love to connect with you to hear what you thought of *Hooked* and share in your successes with storytelling.

Please connect with us in any or all of these ways!

www.facebook.com/onethousandand1

@onethousandand1 — use the hashtag #hooked

www.youtube.com/user/learnstorytelling

hooked@onethousandandone.com.au

Looking forward to connecting with you.

Gabrielle & Yamini

www.onethousandandone.com.au

Learn more with practical advice from our experts

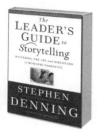

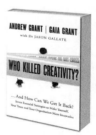